Level-Up
Leadership: Six Factor Leadership

Level-Up *Leadership:* Six Factor Leadership

Second Edition

Leadership Lessons *from* over Twenty Years of Training Executives

Dr. Michael J. Provitera

Copyright © July 25, 2023 by Dr. Michael J. Provitera, Founder of Motivational Leadership Training located in Fort Myers, Florida, USA.

All rights reserved. No part of this book may be reproduced or transmitted in any form or by any means, electronic or mechanical, including photocopy, recording, or any information storage and retrieval system, without prior permission from the publisher (except by reviewers who may quote brief passages).

Second Edition (NOTE: This edition comes with a Spanish version produced by Steven Trujillo, Executive Producer and Co-author residing in the country of Ecuador.

Printed in the United States of America on July 25, 2023

Paperback (Electronic Version Available Now)
Level Up Leadership: Six Factor Leadership
Authored by Dr. Michael J Provitera
Cover Design Illustrated by Daniela Frongia
Edited by Janet Provitera
6" x 9" (15.24 x 22.86 cm)
Black & White on Cream paper
222 pages
ISBN-13: 978-1722651022
ISBN-10: 1722651024

Published by Motivational Leadership Training, a Proprietary Company created and owned by the founder Dr. Michael Provitera

This book is dedicated to Janet and Lauren, my daughters. Two of the greatest young ladies on earth.

I also dedicate this book to my girlfriend Jean. Jean is the spirit of hope in my life. She has a heart of gold and contributes to my happiness every day. Jean's mother, Angelina, did a great job of raising Jean to be a strong, smart, and God-Fearing woman.

Contents

Acknowledgements……………………………………7
Preface……………………………………………………10
Foreword (TBA)……………………………………...14

Chapters

Introduction………………………………………………..16
Chapter One: Professional Communication and
Authentic Leadership……………………………………21
Chapter Two: Decision Making………………………35
Chapter Three: Motivating People…………………51
Chapter Four: Managing People……………………...77
Chapter Five: Core Leadership Principles…………109
Chapter Six: Leadership and Change………………123
Final Thoughts…………………………………………142
Complimentary Case Studies………………………...153
Case 1: The Wizard of Oz and Level-UP Leadership
Case 2: Level-Up Leadership Case (Featured Case)
Case 3: The Last Castle Video Case: Applying Leadership Theory
Case 4: Facing the Giants and Leadership

Acknowledgments

The City of North Miami participants of the Leadership Certification Course, participants from seminars from around the world, and the undergraduate and graduate students at Barry University that pasted through my classroom----whether online or in-class. Most importantly, this book is my tribute to **Sister Linda Bevilacqua, OP, PhD, and President of Barry University** (Her great leadership is an inspiration to so many students, faculty, and administrators), and all the Adrian Dominican Sisters-----especially Sister Mary Tindel, Sister Mary Fran, Sister Evelyn, Sister Myra, and Sister Sara---and the Adrian Dominican Order created by the great Saint Dominic which led to the origin of Barry University in 1940. A special adoration to Mary Lach, Director of Associate life for the Adrian Dominican Sisters, who stood by my side while I labored through the writing of this book----a dear friend and colleague.

I would also like to thank the administrators of the School of Professional and Career Education----Dr. Andrea Keener (a wonderful support of faculty throughout her leadership at Barry U.), Dr. Marilyn Marousek, and Dr. Christopher and Gerry Starratt who became supportive colleagues when becoming an Adrian Dominican Associate----all of these special administrators make my training and teaching available to thousands of students and seminar participants over the past fifteen years. Special admiration to Bob Scully, John Rushing, Judy Brown, Stephen Sussman, and Al Carreras, true professionals that helped me with encouragement and camaraderie. One last but not least person, Dr. Gordon DiPaolo, he helped me send books to 100 orphans in Tanzania, Africa.

Preface

On January 3rd, 2003, a professor of management from Saint Peter's College where he was a professor of management for 3 years, now called Saint Peter's University, made a transition to Barry University in Miami, Florida USA. Over the years, Dr. Providera had taught various management courses at both the undergraduate and graduate level. He also conducted management consulting at leading organizations and universities and has conducted management and leadership training worldwide.

He found that employees are motivated to perform at their peak level for various reasons. While we cannot adequately define all the reasons employees choose to put forth effort and at other times choose not to, we can identify some common motivational tools that will help us increase our employee motivation at work. Several motivational theories have paved the way to help managers understand this important but illusive concept called "Motivation."

For example, if we ascertain a new job in a city or town that we would like to work in and this job fits our expectations for our knowledge and skills, we will probably feel—at least for the moment—highly motivated. However, after time passes and our initial feelings are simple memories of the past we then look for other reasons to sustain our motivation. It is here that the motivational theories can help employees stay motivated. Just by understanding the underlying concepts, one begins to feel that they can secure a better future for oneself and his or her family (or significant other). The reason being each employee wants to succeed and desires to grow and learn. If managers can anticipate, plan, and develop an employee from the onset then there is a strong possibility that the employee will continue to be on the road to success.

Some employees will have a low desire for monetary compensation or may not need cash flow due to wealthy parents or old money. If this is your case, congratulations, but if it is not, then you, like many others, will have to find ways to motivate yourself. In the first case, if money is not a motivating factor, then how do we motivate you? The answer is simple. This person is going to need sincere recognition, perquisites such as travel assignments, a corner office with a window, golf outings, etc. In the latter case, money may be an important motivating factor to secure food and shelter for his or her family. Remember when you first lived away from home. You had feelings of freedom, security, success, and most of all independence where the cornerstones of the new endeavors lay. Some people are motivated by money and some by internal gratification and it is interesting that many of us are motivated by both tangible and intangible rewards. All the perquisites (or intrinsic rewards) in the world will not feed your family so managers must provide a combination of both incentives to motivate employees.

Some people, however, feel uncomfortable receiving compliments. They may come from a family or culture that would prefer to fend for themselves and feel that compliments are not important. For these employees, managers must offer a more challenging job with growth opportunity in lieu of compliments. In short, employees are motivated based on what they perceive their needs to be and not always the way the organization or managers sees their needs to be.

So how do you motivate your employees? First, people learn how to motivate themselves and others by learning about the motivational theories that have helped us understand employee motivation for several decades. Second, people learn how to motivate themselves and others by applying the theories that you feel comfortable with and work for you. You may choose a part of one motivational theory and a part of another, combine several, or come up with your own. This is encouraged. Motivational theories expand our mind and create an ongoing thinking process in which once learned we are never the same again. Third, by creating a culture that fosters motivation. So let us look at some general ideas of motivation and how it relates to leading people.

The SIX FACTOR LEADERSHIP concept was coined and became a way to train executives not only on the art of motivation, but most important, on leading effectively while motivating followers.

Overview of the Six Factors

In my search to find compelling examples of what can be accomplished when people work for and report to a great leader to help their organization, community, or institution, the components of leadership that are most effective stood out, among others. This is not to say that there are other factors of leadership that are important. My focus is on six factors that are essential for leadership success.

What are these six critical factors that determine the success in leading people? What are the core elements that made leaders become effective at their task to motivate staff and followers? There are, of course, a number of forces that affect the leading of people: task at hand, follower readiness level, and leadership style.

I am convinced that the true leaders of today can find attributes in the SIX FACTORS that relate to them. I believe that the leadership strategies that enable managers to become great at what they do are a set of principles that, while seem very common, are not applied as often as they should be. The underlying ingredients of SIX FACTOR LEADERSHIP are expressed in these six factors that I have found to create, enhance, and continuously develop leaders.

1. Professional Communication
2. Decision Making
3. Motivating People
4. Managing People
5. Leading People
6. Leadership and Change

Foreword

By Mateo Gomez, M.B.A., Miami, Florida, USA

Many words are a result of leadership: Administration. Operations. Supervision. Leadership, and Supervision, to name a few. Words that all relate to management consulting. Words that sound controlling. Words that all relate to credibility, intelligence, and order as organizations, and people, build their brand. Words, such as the ones above, are certainly talked about in an MBA class, but what relevance do they truly have to your career? First, and foremost, they are words that automatically create a power structure in your mind. Second, Leadership and Management are two words that could be used almost interchangeably. However, they are not necessarily the same. It is important to remember, though, that to have effective management, you need a good leader or a good group of leaders. Let me take you through my thought process behind my thinking – one based on logic and ideas, and the other based upon my own personal experience.

As professionals, we all might start at the bottom, trying to become the best person that we can in our company, and eventually get to that management position that that bachelor's or master's degree helped us ascertain. But just because we got to that management position, that does not mean that we are leaders. It is important to remember that even though a title might promise us a position or at least a promotion, it does not mean that we learn all the skills needed in order to be effective. Then how do you learn those skills that will build our personal brand? One way is to listen carefully and critically think. Your knowledge is comprehensive and began when you were five years old. At that time, we listened to the people around us. Now, it is important to listen (and read) about theories and models of management that are effective. Learn from other leaders, your co-workers, and your customers. But most importantly, listen to your thoughts and feelings because this builds your authentic leadership presence.

Let me explain. I am not a huge feelings person, but this is when you actually need to listen to what is inside you. Why be in a management position if the group you work with does not enjoy going to work or they do not want to talk to you? Remember when that was you that did not want to go to work to deal with those folks in management positions? Or remember when they spoke to you in code? You probably what they meant but you felt that you were alienated. Thus, my personal view is to learn from your experience.

We have all been there. We have been that student, that professor, that teacher, or that mentor to others. We have been that person starting fresh in that entry-level job, but we have also managed others. Learn from when you were that student and see what worked and did not work for you. Know the difference between what should stay in theory-form and what should actually be applied. Simply listen to what you feel deep inside.

What about the other skills? Here is another tip – be grateful. Thank the people around you. Thank the ones that are there when fires need to be extinguished. Thank your team. Thank the ones that taught you what you know and got you to the place that you are. Thank the ones giving you feedback. Even thank the ones that you feel don't appreciate what you do. This keeps us humble. It helps us remember that we need others to get us to where we need to be. We need others to help us exceed and be those leaders that we were meant to be. It helps us to remember that we are not only the substance of that degree hanging on the wall or the job title that we have. We are humans and we need other humans. It helps us remember that we are replaceable and that anyone can take our position. Thus, we need to be grateful.

As a leader, you have your list of tips and tricks. Attributes that you tallied up about what you liked and did not like when you worked for someone. Use those as milestones on how you should be in your leadership position. That is the greatest tip I can give you. Before there is any professional consulting done, listen to yourself and be grateful for that knowledge and the people that taught you what you know.

Remember to return the favor. Be that mentor. Be the one that gives feedback and help others get to where they want to go. Be a consultant to anyone that knocks on your door and wants your opinion on something or is seeking advice. Be a "person" to them and don't talk to them as a computer. Be that trustworthy person and be that mentor and leader that every successful person has once had. Make that person you work with want to come to work and want to learn. Be that educator and teacher of what is right and wrong. Be that leader in that management position that is a role model for others to follow.

Management does not have to be a hierarchy triangle. It might be like that on paper or to the HR department, but don't let it feel like that during your day-to-day work with your team. Now that you have my tips on leading yourself and others, you are ready to make that profound changes that you will learn in Dr. Michael Provitera's book "Level UP Leadership: Six Factor Leadership." I wish I read this book when I was studying leadership in my MBA program. It is a practical appellation of management and leadership concepts captured in six simple, but profound, steps. Each step is easy to apply to oneself and one's organization.. I hope that you enjoy this book as much as I do. I often refer to the book before meetings and when I meet with clients. I strongly recommend that you continue reading and make this book one of your references to your successful management career.

Favorite Quote:

"Fat Belly Never Knows Hunger."

—Bruce Lee

Introduction
Six Factor Leadership

Six factor leadership is based upon six pillars. The six pillars hold up the model of leadership that I designed in a leadership certification course for a prominent city in Florida. I have used the seminars individually for years but when charged with creating a certification course in leadership; these are the six factors that I felt are the most relevant. You may be asking, "How does this relate to Trait Theory?" It does not. However, Trait Theory is codified with several traits that leadership should or could possess to be successful. I encourage scholars and practitioners to explore more in-depth. Here is what trait theory is about. Kendra Cherry and Steven Gans, a Medical Doctor, wrote an article titled "Understanding the Trait Theory of Leadership: A Closer Look at Key Leadership Traits," on May 7, 2018. They state that:

The trait theory of leadership focuses on identifying different personality traits and characteristics that are linked to successful leadership across a variety of situations. This line of research emerged as one of the earliest types of investigations into the nature of effective leadership and is tied to the "great man" theory of leadership first proposed by Thomas Carlyle in the mid-1800s.

Cherry and Gans feel that according to Carlyle, extraordinary leaders shape history. This ability to lead is something that people are simply born with, Carlyle believed, and could not be developed. Carlyle's ideas inspired early research on leadership, which almost entirely focused on inheritable traits. Some of the implications of the trait theory of leadership are that:

- Certain traits produce certain patterns of behavior
- These patterns are consistent across different situations
- People are born with these leadership traits

Cherry and Gans point out important research on the Trait Theory of Leadership. Later research on the Trait Theory of Leadership includes:

- **1948**—Ralph Melvin Stogdill's studies suggest that leadership is the result of the interaction between the individual and the social situation and not the result of a predefined set of traits.

- **1974**—Stodgill conducts additional studies, which find that both traits and situational variables contribute to leadership.

- **1980s**—James M. Kouzes and Barry Z. Posner survey more than 1,500 managers and find that the top four traits associated with good leadership are being honest, forward-looking, inspiring, and competent. Kouzes and Posner refer to these four characteristics as "being credible."

The fact of the matter is that the six traits that I focus on will help any executive, manager, or aspiring leader reach the upper echelons of organizations, institutions, universities, and the public sector. Therefore, explore the trait theory of leadership and add the traits that you would like to develop to your reputation of leadership competencies.

Cherry and Gans found that there are some traits most commonly associated with great leadership include the following. Here is their list and there is a plethora more available to you for review.

Intelligence and Action-Oriented Judgment: Great leaders are smart and make choices that move the group forward.

Eagerness to Accept Responsibility: Strong leaders take on responsibility and do not pass the blame onto others. They stand by their success and take ownership of their mistakes.

Task Competence: A great leader is skilled and capable. Members of the group are able to look to the leader for an example of how things should be done.

Understanding Followers and Their Needs: Effective leaders pay attention to group members and genuinely care about helping them succeed. They want each person in the group to succeed and play a role in moving the entire group forward.

People Skills: Excellent interpersonal skills are essential for leading effectively. Great leaders know how to interact well with other leaders as well as with team members.

Need for Achievement: Strong leaders have a need to succeed and help the group achieve their goals. They genuinely care about the success of the group and are committed to helping the group reach these milestones.

Capacity to Motivate People: A great leader knows how to inspire others and motivate them to do their best.

Courage and Resolution: The best leaders are brave and committed to the goals of the group. They do not hide from challenges.

Perseverance: Strong leaders stick with it, even when things get difficult, or the group faces significant obstacles.

Trustworthiness: Group members need to be able to depend upon and trust the person leading them.

Decisiveness: A great leader is capable of making a decision and is confident in his or her choices.

Self-Confidence: Many of the best leaders are extremely self-assured. Because they are confident in themselves, followers often begin to share this self-belief.

Assertiveness: A great leader is able to be direct and assertive without coming off as overly pushy or aggressive.

Adaptability and Flexibility: Effective leaders are not stuck in a rut. They are able to think outside of the box and adapt quickly to changing situations.

Emotional Stability: In addition to being dependable overall, strong leaders are able to control their emotions and avoid overreactions.

Creativity: Perhaps most importantly, great leaders not only possess their own creativity, but they are also able to foster creativity among members of the group.

There are *four case studies **FREE*** that accompany this book; contact the author for the teaching notes. Now, let us focus on my Six Factor Leadership.

Dr. Michael Provitera (All Rights Reserved and Credit Given to Authors Above).

1

Pillar One -
Professional Communication and Authentic Leadership

"The greatest problem with communication is the assumption that it has taken place." -George Bernard Shaw

INTRODUCTION

The Worst Leaders according to a Harvard Business Review article titled "Ten Fatal Flaws That Derail Leaders," Jack Zenger Joseph Folkman, CEO and President, accordingly, of Zenger/Folkman, which a leadership development consultancy. Zenger and Folkman found that the worst leaders:

Lack energy and enthusiasm. They see new initiatives as a burden, rarely volunteer, and fear being overwhelmed. One such leader was described as having the ability to "suck all the energy out of any room."

Accept their own mediocre performance. They overstate the difficulty of reaching targets so that they look good when they achieve them. They live by the mantra "Under-promise and over-deliver."

Lack clear vision and direction. They believe their only job is to execute. Like a hiker who sticks close to the trail, they are fine until they come to a fork.

Have poor judgment. They make decisions that colleagues and subordinates consider to be not in the organization's best interests.

Do not collaborate. They avoid peers, act independently, and view other leaders as competitors. As a result, the very people whose insights and support they need set them adrift.

Do not walk the talk. They set standards of behavior or expectations of performance and then violate them. They are perceived as lacking integrity.

Resist new ideas. They reject suggestions from subordinates and peers. Good ideas are not implemented, and the organization is stuck.

Do not learn from mistakes. They may make no more mistakes than their peers may, but they fail to use setbacks as opportunities for improvement, hiding their errors and brooding about them instead.

Lack interpersonal skills. They make sins of both commission (they are abrasive and bullying) and omission (they are aloof, unavailable, and reluctant to praise).

Fail to develop others. They focus on themselves to the exclusion of developing subordinates, causing individuals and teams to disengage.

Communicate a Winning Attitude

Ken Blanchard is one of most well-known academics in the extant literature that has mastered the art of blending theoretical concepts and practical application. He was the first management scholar/practitioner to come up with a formula or recipe for management and leadership success.

For decades, he set up a prescriptive management platform that set the stage for practicing managers.

But that all changed when he introduced attitude into leadership development. He began a seminar by asking people to get up, wander around for about 30 seconds and greet as many people as possible, but he asked people to greet each other in a very special way, he asked the participants to greet them as if they are unimportant and that they are looking for someone that is much more important to talk to! He would say, "So go ahead, greet them as if they are unimportant!"

Then suddenly, after about a minute or so he would say, "Stop where you are but do not sit down!"

He would then ask them to greet each other for about 30 seconds, but this time, greet each other as if they are a long-lost friend that you are really glad to see!

What do you think the outcome was? Rhetorical question. Many people did not know how to treat people as unimportant but went along with it while others treated people with massive compassion when asked to.

The backlash was swift and predictable. People realized that communication is all about attitude and leaders with a good attitude can spread that feeling in contagion.

Julian Treasure in a Youtube.com video titled "How to speak so that people want to listen," creates a presence on stage that is worth viewing. He actually cares about leadership communication so much that he asks the following questions:

Have you ever talked, but felt like nobody is listening? Here is Julian Treasure to help you fix that. As the sound expert demonstrates some useful vocal exercises and shares tips on how to speak with empathy, he offers his vision for a sonorous world of listening and understanding.

Today, leadership can be taught free. Universities are vying for seat capacity and students cannot get enough of it. The knowledge today is so abundant that the four-year degree has replaced the High School Diploma. High school students are not wondering if they should go to college; it is now WHERE? However, the outcome has been bleak. In my earlier writing as a motivational expert, I found that 50 percent of college students do graduate and find work in their field, while 25 percent do not, and the other 25 percent are working jobs that may not be aligned with their major just to pay the bills. The interesting point here that is seldom made is that it does not matter what college you go to either---students at high-end Ivy League universities are vying for jobs among the masses looking. The key for the college graduate or anyone leading their life is to make connections, keep connections, use connections, and never turn down an opportunity to make your next connection.

Richard Boyatzis, a Distinguished University Professor, and a Professor in the Departments of Organizational Behavior in Psychology and Cognitive Science at a leading university, offers a course free on a leading free-course platform. He begins one of his lectures by having participants write down the good, bad, and ugly of past leaders. Then jumps to what it takes to be a great leader. One thing that stood out for me was Boyatzis' idea that "Command and Control" does not work anymore. Instead, he suggests that leaders now "Ask and Inspire." Easy to suggest but hard to do. Nevertheless, worth the effort. By asking followers to do things that they want to do, leaders will elicit a real response to becoming better and more effective at what they do. Inspiring is something we think about as we look in the mirror and decide whether we have leadership skills or not. If we feel we do, we feel inspired; if we feel we do not, we have to go out and seek out people to inspire us to be all that we can be. Commanding may work in the short run for a while but will lose steam fast and in the end, controlling only leads to resentment. Some followers may leave with a feeling that they were glad they were controlled because they ended up successful, but most will feel oppressed and micro-managed.

An important assumption of leadership is that we map our story. Storytellers at the Academy of Management asked a group to map their story. The stories heard were so illuminating that people bonded and got to know each other very well. Some asked critical questions about the stories but most were enamored and impressed while others surprised and intrigued.

By asking the participants in my training sessions to write their story in a few sentences has led to most pertinent and amazing discussions while training executives. One leader was pulled over by a police officer because his plate had a "Z" that looked like the number seven because the bottom of the Z was not fully showing. Everything else on the plate matched the police log so the man was pulled over, arrested and taken into custody. Once the officer found out that the plate was misleading, he reflected on the person arrested. The man was so nice and reassuring that this was a complete mistake and went along with the police officer in a polite manner. The arresting officer noticed a great personality and leadership potential, that he was offered a job. He is now a senior executive in law enforcement at a level that would ask and inspire many. Story telling draws our inner thoughts and helps us personalize ourselves leading to a topic worth noting titled "Authentic Leadership."

*"**Authentic leadership is leading adaptively from your core, choosing who you're most inspired to be to serve the greatest good in this moment."*** — *Henna Inam*

In an article by Martin Gruber, a professor at New York University, Manhattan, New York USA, stated that:

"In order to lead better, leaders and academics have turned to the idea of authentic leadership. A leadership model, which believes that genuine leadership that bases its decisions on values, can guide people towards the greater good."

Presenting an Authentic Leadership Guide, one thing that executives will find special is this brilliant section of the article, captured as an excerpt (refer to full article for a complete guide to

Authentic Leadership):

A year after *Authentic Leadership* was published, the conversation got busier, and the Gallup Leadership Institute of the University of Nebraska-Lincoln held its inaugural summit on Authentic Leadership Development. In 2007, George's *True North* went further to explain who's an authentic leader and what leaders can do to be more authentic, creating a concept that could be further refined, but also tested.

The book restated the idea that leadership is not something you are born with, but that ***authentic leadership, especially, requires constant development and growth***. George developed an idea of leadership as a journey, with three distinct phases:

Phase 1: In the first part of your journey, you prepare yourself for the leadership.

Phase 2: In the second phase, you start leading by taking on new challenges until you reach the 'peak' of leadership.

Phase 3: In the final part of the leadership journey, you start seeking opportunities to spread your leadership wisdom to others and give back to the community, even though the learning process continues.

Authentic leadership is an entire graduate course at New York University. None of us was born yesterday and we all have a life story: some should be held close to the chest while others should be told. The journey to authentic leadership begins with understanding the story of your life. Your life story provides the context for your experiences, and through it, you can find the inspiration to make an impact in the world.

Level up leadership is about communicating professionally as a leader. No one person can master communication alone. There has to be an audience. Followership is the key to great leadership because without followers, there is no one to lead. A strong emphasis is on building a customer service presence and one of the best to turn to is Ken Blanchard. Ken came up with Situational Service, a component that models his leadership training. Once you master Situational Service as a leader, you can help your followers follow suit.

Upside down leadership was once uncovered in a Business Horizon article with a similar title that places the customer on top. The City of North Miami surprised me when they established this idea before I introduced it to them. Placing the customer on top not only helps the organization focus on the heart and soul of the organization but it causes a commonly known leadership model titled "Servant Leadership" to surface. This model has helped executives turn the cards from receiver to server----and serving not only the customer but also staff and for stakeholders to become the norm. The best example is Johnson and Johnson Corporation when they took Tylenol off every shelf after a few people found the product to be faulty. Placing precedence in this order customers, employees, communities, and then stockholders. Who is really at the top of this totem pole? Look at what they present on their website:

Robert Wood Johnson, chairman from 1932 to 1963 and a member of the Company's founding family, drafted our credo himself in 1943, just before Johnson & Johnson became a publicly traded company. This was long before anyone ever heard the term "corporate social responsibility." Our credo is more than just a moral compass. We believe it is a recipe for business success. The fact that Johnson & Johnson is one of only a handful of companies that have flourished through more than a century of change is proof of that.

Boyatzis has this leadership factor right – he argues that each of us has a model of leadership inside us and we have to look for the opportunity to seek people who bring out the best in us, light us up, and help to inspire us to bring our all. You have the opportunity to make the necessary changes in your life that will provide you with a road map, a guide, a yellow-brick-road. Find it!

"Be who [you are] meant to be and you will set the world on fire."
— Catherine of Siena

Authentic leadership is really, what all leaders should aspire to be. Ann Fudge, Chairman and CEO, of Young and Rubicam once said that we all have a spark of leadership in us. The challenge is to understand ourselves well enough to discover where we can use our leadership gifts to serve others.

Leaders need to know both internal and external customers. Paul Hersey, a behaviorist, once said that all leaders need to perform in a functional way, but it is the interaction with followers and customers that wins their long-term loyalty. Dissatisfied customers tell at least twice as many friends about bad experiences then they tell about good ones. The same thing goes with leadership. Do your followers like being around you or do they avoid you until it is necessary for them to engage with you? Paul Hersey created a cornerstone of leadership by building on Blake and Mouton's Organizational Grid. From there, he developed Situational Leadership, a model that has stood the test of time. He had an ingenious way of taking something that works in one area and applying it to other areas----for example, Situational Service. He did this by providing information and ensuring satisfaction to customers or followers. He then broke service style into two categories: Directive Behavior and Supportive Behavior. This will be talked about later when I introduce Situational Leadership, but you can see how Paul was able to capture the hearts and minds of followers. For more on this idea, refer to his book entitled "Situational Service":

Professional communication as a leader involves being a great listener. Some say that we have two ears and one mouth and that is because we should be listening twice as much as we talk. Become an empathetic and reflective listener. Understand the feelings of the person that you are engaged with and reflect by delving into the details of the people that you care about. Paul Hersey expects leaders to remember that there may be a regressive style to leadership. This happens when communication between the leader and follow or customer slips. When this happens, leaders can adapt their style to adhere to the situation.

SUMMARY

Professional communication and Authentic Leadership are probably the most important attributes of a leader. Why? Well, primarily, all leaders have to communicate through various channels, and they have to do this well. Secondly, being an authentic leader goes to the saying "Be Real." We do not want to be fake, less transparent, or stoic as a leader.

CONCLUSION

Remember that every morning in Africa, a gazelle wakes up. It knows that it must outrun the fastest lion, or it will be killed and eaten. Also, every morning in Africa, a lion wakes up. It knows it must run faster than the slowest gazelle or it will starve. Therefore, it does not matter whether you are a lion or gazelle-----when the sun comes up tomorrow, you better be leading. Do not miss your leadership moment! Get up every day with a complete enthusiasm of success and prosperity.

KEY TAKEAWAYS

1. Take the time out to develop a monologue of a story that you can tell----stories linger in people's minds and add value. Stand straight, level off on your two feet, shoulders back, lean in to make a point, move around, and raise your voice on occasion to drive a point home.

2. Always speak from the heart. People often say that people have a good heart, but the heart is directly correlated with the brain. Think before you respond, stay positive, get to the core of the question and answer it in detail but do not go off on a tangent.

3. Remember body language, tone, eye contact, and most of all, a sincere desire to want to communicate.

4. Create a positive presence everywhere you go. Hold your head up high and have a chip on your shoulder. Do not be cocky but understand your self-worth and have high self-efficacy [i.e., a feeling that you can do well in any industry in any position in any city or state].

5. Stand up for what is right in the world. We should sometimes think about other people more than we think of ourselves. I sometimes think of a "Dog Theory," – Doesn't your dog love you, and, in some cases, love you more than they love themselves? We may not want to go that far to

think of dog-mentality but there is something to be said about why people love their pets so much. Remember that your job as a leader is to give away your knowledge and strength about leading people. It is not your job to know what they do with it but to hope that they do great things. However, do not be too aggressive; be assertive. State your opinion but be open minded toward your followers' viewpoints and stay in control of your thoughts at all times. Stay away from the martini lunches and office parties---if you do indulge, indulge with caution and know your limit. Say very little but listen closely. Leadership communication more about listening than it is about speaking. Leading others is so profound that people will hang on your every word and watch your body contact as if you are the most important leader in the world---so why not be the best leader you can be!

2

Pillar Two –
Decision Making

"The advantages of having decisions made by groups are often lost because of powerful psychological pressures that arise when the members work closely together, share the same set of values and, above all, face a crisis situation that puts everyone under intense stress." -Irving L. Janis

What are the advantages of making decisions ourselves versus making them in teams and groups? Control freaks may like the ability to control the situation from the get-go and leave people wondering what just happened. There may also be a personal choice that is expounded onto others for selfish reasons because there may be a perceived lack of the need to please others. However, making decisions by yourself is great when you are alone and the captain of your own ship but even captains use tools to navigate the treacherous waters of life.

The decision-making in a group setting can bring diversity and insight among the followers that the leader may have overlooked. There can also be a balance between what the followers want and what the leader needs. Most importantly, you are combining the years of experience tenfold----the more people in the room adds multiple experience. Ronald Reagan, one our Republican Presidents that acted more like a democrat at times, would ask as many people as possible for their opinion when making a decision but then he would make it himself.

Groupthink is an idea that often settles the cause to make decisions alone but even so, groups are still making effective decisions. Therefore, as a leader, you have to decide on what type of decision maker you are!

Decisions must be made the way you want them to be made as a leader.

In the Lost At Sea exercise, I gather people together to see if they can decide upon what they would need to survive. Many people fail to decide properly and in a real situation would die at sea. When was the last time you had a decision that was so crucial that you needed to make it right or face the consequences?

Groupthink addresses the psychological factors that can make or break effective decisions. Think about how people react in situations. Going to the movies – seeing a movie that you do not want to see but going because the group is going. This once happened to me as a boy when the Exorcist came out. My friend Wayne's Mom took Wayne and me to the movie. I almost jumped out of my seat, was in a captive audience situation, and never outlived the feelings of trauma affecting me today. How has groupthink impacted your company?

NASA had its fallouts with Groupthink, and this has been well documented to provide an example of the fatalities of it. CRM Films capture this example in a great video worth watching. Such things as direct pressure, illusion of vulnerability, and rationalization are introduced as direct causes of groupthink.

Irving Janis, in Britannica, is introduced as the father of groupthink:

The theory of groupthink was first developed by the social psychologist Irving Janis in his classic 1972 study, Victims of Groupthink: A Psychological Study of Foreign-Policy Decisions and Fiascoes, which focused on the psychological mechanism behind foreign policy decisions such as the Pearl Harbor bombing, the Vietnam War, and the Bay of Pigs invasion.

Janis found that people could make what he called clearly hopeless courses of actions. We all strive to please ourselves along with others. This has been ingrained in us since childhood. Some people do this all the time and find themselves either alone or out of a job.

A successful team player knows when to shoot the ball in the hoop or pass it without having to contemplate his or her decision for more than split-second. This type of thinking will help team players remain integral parts of the group while still managing themselves and helping the group decide.

Daniel Goleman is an internationally known psychologist who lectures frequently to professional groups, business audiences, and on college campuses. As a science journalist, Goleman reported on the brain and behavioral sciences for The New York Times for many years. He argues that we all want to belong to a secure family of some sought. The first five years of our life, if we did not view the crib as prison bars, before we eventually had a crib of our own, help us to feel secure to handle the roller coaster we now call life. Abraham Maslow captured this feeling of belonging along the pyramid of his Hierarchy of Needs model.

"Reality is fearsome, but experience tells us more fearsome yet is evading it." — Bill Moyers (The Public Mind)

Leaders can pose questions to significantly impact future course direction. A book titled "The Goal" was a story about an Operations Management Guru, E. I. Goldratt that asked questions throughout the book at pertinent times to initiate action. I never can forget the image of a man with black pants and a white shirt with no tie. Here is what it says on the Amazon.com platform:

Written in a fast-paced thriller style, *The Goal* is the gripping novel which is transforming management thinking throughout the Western world. The author has been described by Fortune as a 'guru to industry' and by Businessweek as a 'genius'. It is a book to recommend to your friends in industry - even to your bosses - but not to your competitors.

Another colleague and friend of mine Hal Gregerson ran a full day seminar titled "The Questions We Ask."

In his book titled "The Innovator's DNA," Hal opens up with questions that leaders need to ask. The book itself consists of five "discovery skills" that separate true innovators from the rest of us. However, Hal expects leaders to ask questions and ask followers what questions they are going to ask or asked at the last meeting. Decision-making is about asking the right questions. Let me give you an example:

Mary asks: John, would you tell me how the time value of money works? I just do not seem to understand it.

John says: "Well, if you lend me $20 and I give you back a twenty-dollar bill next year, did you lose any money?"

Mary says: "No."

John says: "What the bank's paying in interest today?"

Mary says: "Oh, I see what you mean."

We do not always have to answer the question and we may sometimes be better off eluding to the right answer instead.

Executives sometimes bring in experts to share new decision-making skills. Jamie Diamond left Merrill Lynch for J.P. Morgan and was paid $20,000,000 to not take any of his staff for two years. Jamie Diamond also made the decision to make pay cuts to senior executives to offset losses and maintain the current salaries of the lower-level employees. Decisions are hard to make at times but given the current situation, people sometimes understand the necessity of them.

The creative side to decision making is crucial. With a broad and in-depth investigation and preparation, the leader can begin the incubator process. This may provide insight that may not be easily acquired any other way.

Strong-minded leaders may want to pull themselves out of meetings at times to let the group make decisions without them.
Creative people are not only intelligent, they also are persistent. It took Thomas Edison 5000 times to create the lightbulb and his critics thought he would never be able to create it. Instead of halting his decision to create the lightbulb, he reacted by saying to a young journalist that he had found 4,999 times how *NOT* to create the light bulb prior to his astounding invention. Light swept across the rest of the world swiftly and immediately following his

invention.

What had happened to cause such quick decision making once the light bulb was created?

Simply put, people caught on and instead of locking out the idea of light, they locked on to not only the possibility, but also the reality of it. People using other forms of light had been blind-sided by the new invention, with a root cause that appeared almost laughable—if the consequences weren't so much in need. Meanwhile, the whale hunting and oil lamp became obsolete.

An important concept of decision making that has been touted by academic scholars for many years has taken a back seat to the executive. Being a back seat driver may mean this type of decision-making resurfaces in the corporate boardrooms of America and throughout the world.

Proposed by the US Nobel-laureate economist Herbert Simon (1916-2001) in his 1982 book 'Models of Bounded Rationality and Other Topics in Economics, this model realizes that humans have limitations, and this constrains the rational component of decision making. In effect, leaders may not try to maximize a goal due to a number of reasons. Perhaps they did not have time to look at all the alternatives available to them or are too dynamic and allow too many changes all at once. The key for all executives with this model is we all tend to "Satisfice." We select the best option because it is the best in the lot but not because it is the optimal choice. Leaders need to be aware of the fact that satisficing behavior may be inherent in all decision-making processes at any stage.

Another pertinent component of decision-making comes from Steve Kerr and his famous article titled "On the Folly of Rewarding A While Hoping for B." Steve argued that we hope for long-term growth, yet we look at quarterly earnings. Why? One reason is that quarterly earnings are at the forefront of hostile takeovers. There are investors just waiting for a bad quarter or two so that they can raid a company and try to do better. Another is one of my favorites. We hope for teamwork, but we reward individual effort. Teamwork unfolded like a house of cards while I was at Salomon Brothers in Tampa, Florida. We tried a teamwork model and put loads of money and effort into the platform. It backfired because we really needed to focus on individual effort. Teamwork is great on the ball field, but it has not yet made a big enough splash in the workplace---although attempts are and will continue to be made.

Kerr argued that we set stretch goals but focus on making the numbers and quotas instead. Companies often try to downsize, right size, delay, and restructure yet they reward adding staff for adding budgetary items. Another best one is emphasis on "Total Quality" yet rewarding shipping on schedule—even with defects. Finally, a component that has true limitations in corporate America: worldwide, universities, and in institutions. Hoping for candor and surfacing bad news early while rewarding the reporting of good news whether it is good or not---is something known today as "fake news."

Based on the advice of William Bratton, the police

commissioner of New York City, in an article called "Tipping Point Leadership," by W. Chan Kim and Renee Mauborgne, from the April 2003 issue, Kim and Mauborgne posited that:

"Yes, the odds were against him because the New York City Police Department had a 2$ Billion budget and a workforce of 35,000 police officers, and this was notoriously difficult to manage."

Three tenets are worth noting in the article:

1) In any organization, once the beliefs and energies of a critical mass of people are engaged, conversation to a new idea will spread like an epidemic.
2) Leaders like Bratton do not need extra resources to reach the tipping point. They concentrate resources where they are needed and where the likely payoffs are greatest.
3) Bratton solves the motivation problem by singling out the key influencers. They act like kingpins in bowling: when you hit them just right, all the pins topple over.

Decision-making is an important component of leadership.

Leaders typically make decision-making errors. Our minds are so congested with facts, figures, and things to go, that we often make careless mistakes, put off further analysis, and regret to include new insights---especially with technology increasing at the fastest pace ever today.

As mentioned earlier in Simon's "Bounded Rationality," we tend to *NOT* consider alternatives.

My role as a crisis leadership expert was quickly earned in the training room when I pointed out that incorrect or insufficient decision-making criteria could be fatal. Take for instance 9/11 in New York City or Pearl Harbor or even the Civil War in America. Gathering data and analyzing the outcome occurred too late in the process to be of any use whatsoever. The consequences were an aftermath of complete destruction and fatality.

The bottom line is that many leaders postpone decisions because of the personal, or at times, perceived dissatisfaction with the data found and the analysis done. Leaders need to make quick decisions, and some have to be on the spot in some cases. Universities are notorious for taking an academic year to make a decision and in some cases, this is necessary but, in other cases, quick decisions can be made, and things can get rolling as quickly as possible.

Decision styles also come into play here. There are four decision styles that I talk about in my training: Directive, Analytical, Conceptual, and Behavioral. However, Brent Gleeson, in a Forbes article titled "4 Ways for Leaders to Make a Decision" says:

Business leaders are faced with dozens of decisions that need to be made every day. As our organizations grow, the decisions generally become more frequent; more complicated, and may have ramifications that are more serious. Sometimes it is not about making the right decision, but just making a decision at all.

1) Command decision-making is where leaders make decisions without consulting their teams.

2) Collaborative decision-making is just what it sounds like. Leaders gather their teams and request feedback and insight. The leader still makes the final call but is armed with the proper data to make a more informed decision.

3) Consensus-based decision-making is done more like a democratic vote. Leaders gather their teams, and everyone votes. Majority rules.

4) When surrounded by trusted peers, sometimes the best decision a leader can make is to not be the one to make a certain decision.

    The key here is to use what works best for you and your team. Many leaders are contributing to problems by not controlling the message being heard. A very important component of decision-making is listening.

    Jennifer Lombardo at Study.com uses the same decision styles that I suggest when I train executives. They are concise and to the point. Lombardo states these points:

1) Directive Style: This form of decision-making relies on a rational and autocratic style that results in the employee

using his own knowledge, experience and judgment to choose the best alternative. This type of leader is very rational but thinks mostly about the short-term.

2) Conceptual Style leaders are concerned with long-term results, brainstorming of alternatives, creative approaches to problem solving and taking higher risks.

3) Analytical leaders collect much data and carefully consider alternatives.

4) Behavioral Style leaders may make decisions to help others achieve their goals because they have a deep concern for others.

Which one are you?

Rowe and Boulgarides, in an article in 1983 titled "Management Skills Assessment and Development," found that there are four decision-making styles as mentioned above by Lombardo. Rowe and Boulgardies were the first scholars to dig deeper into the fact that decision styles differ from leadership or management styles. They found this to be true as they considered situational variables, the decision process itself, and a variety of decision style models. The authors conclude that the decision style approach has many applications and is a highly effective management tool. Just think of yourself. If it was up to you, you would make every decision in your life and unfortunately, some of us do. Now, think of the rest of the leaders out there and how they may make decisions. Find your style. As mentioned above, are you analytical, conceptual, behavioral, or directive? Once you know your style, tweak it, define it, analyze it, and change it if you have to. Remember, not every style has to be static and ironclad---we may be considerate of others one day (behavioral) and directive (concerned for our own well-being) the next. In both cases, you as the leader can be right. Learn to find your authentic self and start fresh from there to develop your own leadership style; the style that is the best one for you and the followers that you lead.

    Decision-making is not tantamount to a formula that is universal. The significance of a decision is important; with two important topics: follower commitment and buy-in matters. The starting point is based on how experienced you feel in the particular area. If you are new at Leadership, then shoot for buy-in. If you feel that buy-in exists based on prior experience, then make the decision and disseminate it to your followers. In addition, making a decision alone would have to include the comfort level of followers—some may prefer this type of leader while some may want to provide input. Can people carry out the decision once it has been made? Many people fall short of projects and plans because there is absolutely no follow-through, someone drops the ball, or something bigger comes up---leaving the decision abandoned.

    Creativity in decision-making is paramount to effectiveness. Find ways to keep original ideas by staying current in your field of expertise. Improve your sense of humor by laughing at some of your own mistakes. Leigh Buchanon writes, in INC. Magazine, that "Humor is an under-appreciated tool for engaging employees and building resilient cultures. Many leaders have to work at it." Another thing a creative decision maker must do is take risks and find the best time of the day to work on things that are important to them. If you run into a mental block, walk away, go fishing, and come back later. You will feel rejuvenated.

Think strategically. In my case study "Day in the Life of a CEO," I emphasize conceptual thinking and how to incorporate it into your daily life. The key is to set a compelling rationale and then stick to it---knowing that every great plan has detours and at some point needs tweaking. Remember your mission; whether personal or business, what you do on a day-to-day moment-to-moment basis matters. Think of who you are, what you do, and why you are placed in your position----whatever it may be---personal or professional.

Develop a strong core value system for yourself by matching your own or the organization's vision, mission, and strategy to contribute to your company or division's success.

CONCLUSION

Remember that you are the decision maker at your level and then empower your people below you to make decisions at their level too. Never cut anyone off. Let them talk. Keep the conversation ongoing. Reduce the need to be right all the time. Agree to disagree. See the other person's perspective.

"Leadership is the capacity to translate vision into reality." -Warren Bennis

KEY TAKEAWAYS

1. Earn the trust of your followers, quickly. When first interacting with your followers, express your expertise and a personal experience then shift to them and do not return to your story unless absolutely necessary to drive a point home or close up a loose end.

2. Be painfully honest and direct when it comes to what is expected of your followers. What followers need is someone who will not sugarcoat the decision-making process, but clearly explain the appropriate way to reach the most optimal decision in a collaborative manner. There is no better culture building opportunity than expressing the truth.

3. Be available all the time, at any hour, even in the middle of the night. Do not close up shop and say goodbye at night and on weekends. Let people know that during a crisis that it is imperative that you be there for them. Hillary Clinton as a Presidential Candidate mentioned that she was the one to call at 3AM in the morning---that is powerful leadership. Think of the image and safety and security that sound bite brings.

4. Create a no-jerk policy, which will be covered later in the book but do not give bullies a get out of jail pass—hold

them accountable. Hold people accountable.

5. Control your decision dissemination----do not let people ruin your idea or decision with gossip and rumors. Use both credibility and balance to ensure complete knowledge management.

3

Pillar Three –
Motivating People

"One can choose to go back toward safety or forward toward growth. Growth must be chosen again and again; fear must be overcome again and again." -Abraham Maslow

Bernie Maddoff's fall from grace was as swift and stunning as any in recent memory when it comes to financial scandals.

The worst moment was when the investors that trusted him realized that they had lost fortunes. Some people would argue that his sentence in federal prison was not enough. What motivates people to do things that are out of the ordinary like that? Greed, probably, but there is much more to it than that. People are motivated by an innate core belief system that sets them apart from others.

Since motivation has been and will always be my expertise, I will keep this chapter to a cursory view and stay on point to enhance your leadership presence.

There is a subject that comes to everyone's mind, from academics to motivational gurus, and that is goal-directed behavior. The one thing that both scholars and practitioners believe is that goal setting works. I often start out my seminars with three basic questions that I would like you to think about for a moment:

1) What gets you motivated at work?

2) What factors at work result in your lack of motivation?

3) What do you do for fun that motivates you outside work?

The reason that I ask these questions is because people are stuck in jobs that they do not tend to appreciate, or they like what they do but do not feel appreciated. This is driving the curse of lack of motivation that many leaders are faced with. Therefore, I hinge upon what factors motivate you outside work. Why? Because I know this may be a key motivating factor for people. If someone likes their BMW, they need to pay for gas and upkeep---- only a job can afford such a luxury.

Leaders often ask the question "How do we motivate employees?" The answer is not so simple. We motivate employees by knowing what energizes people, directs, or channels them in a particular direction. Once we have motivated people, then the question remains, how do we sustain or maintain this motivation? The answer to this question is that we sustain motivation by using the dynamics of it and by using some motivational theories. The key that if each of can increase our motivational tools in our toolbox, we can then incorporate them into the workplace and actively engage followers. Abraham Maslow, a motivational guru, once said that: "To him [or her] who has only a hammer, the whole world looks like a nail." Joseph Weizenbaum, a professor of computer science at the Massachusetts Institute of Technology In 1984, once said this. However, for the record, the accurate quote is "If the only tool you have is a hammer, everything looks like a nail."

In Negril, Jamaica, there is a place called Hedonism II. They probably got the name from the word 'hedonism,' which assumes a certain degree of conscious behavior on the part of the individual whereby they make intentional decisions concerning certain motivated actions. A Greek philosopher named Jeremy Bentham coined the term "Hedonic Calculus" as a way of analyzing the pros and cons of acts of behavior back in approximately 1789. Jeremy, from 1748-1832, was an English philosopher, a writer on jurisprudence and a social reformer. He was born in London and went to Queen's College in Oxford. He held that laws should be socially useful and not just reflect the status quo and developed a "hedonic calculus" to estimate the effects of different actions.

Sports psychologists use this idea when talking about no pain no gain…..In Bentham's hedonic calculus, the utility (usefulness) of each action is computed as the algebraic sum of the pleasure to be obtained minus the pain to be caused.

Process theories of motivation are very useful to leaders and executives in the workplace. The theory indicates that performance leads to satisfaction if the individual perceives it to be beneficial. If satisfaction is perceived to be high then the individual will put in the necessary effort, and vice versa, motivation will lapse and, in some cases, get out of control.

All executives should be aware in some way of two prominent process theorists. One, Victor Vroom, and the second, Edwin Locke. All leaders should know new academic scholars that changed the platform of leadership in organizations.

Vroom, in 1964, presented the 'Motivational Force Theory' or 'Expectancy Theory' and Locke, in 1968, introduced the 'Goal Setting Theory'. Do not let the word theory bore you. These are practical models that apply to the workplace and executives use them all the time--- whether tactically or consciously.

Expectancy theory was first used to explain organizational behavior by an American business school professor, Victor Vroom, in his book "Work and Motivation" (1964). Vroom found out that motivation is predetermined by individual factors – skills, knowledge, experience and abilities.

Vroom assumed that followers rationally evaluate various work behaviors and then choose those that they believe will lead to the work-related rewards that they value most----similar to the concept mentioned above by Bentham. Followers consciously calculate the pleasure or pain that they expect to attain or avoid when making a choice.

This theory can be used in so many ways at so many levels. Think about it this way: if you can get your followers to perceive that they can perform at a certain level, if they try it, then they may do it willingly. The key here is to have them handle the task because they want to and not because it is a chore or something, they have to do to keep their job. Second, you have to get the followers to perceive that if they do perform at that certain level that something good will happen. Here is where rewards of some kind or incentives or simply gestures and accolades come into play. However, there is one important point about Vroom's theory that is worth pointing out here. "Do your followers prefer or value the things that will happen if they perform at a certain level?" This is the million-dollar question with the elephant in the room and the whole kitchen sink thrown in. Challenging at best!

Value is a perception that a leader cannot sell or

package in a certain way. It has to come from the individual and cannot be pushed upon them. Well, it could, but that would be coercive leadership; something we will discuss later on.

The point here is simple. Get your followers to perceive that they can perform at a certain level, and once they do perform at that level, reward them in some way. Now, getting them to desire the reward is beyond the scope of this book. However, a good leader can master this trait and followers will appreciate the fact that you do.

Here are five ways in which a leader can apply the motivational force theory:

    1) Determine what outcomes are important to the followers

    2) Know what followers prefer and address individual preferences

    3) Tie the desired outcomes with the certain performance

    4) Ensure that the connection between performance and rewards are communicated well right from the beginning.

    5) Develop a mindset that includes the "What is in it for me?"

People are only motivated by what is in it for them. Even if they are motivated for other reasons, those reasons are still internally driven.

Locke, on the other hand, had his ducks directly in a row: goal set and succeed.

In 1990, Locke and Latham published their seminal work, "A Theory of Goal Setting & Task Performance." In this book, they repeated the need to set specific and difficult goals, while outlining five other characteristics for successful goal setting.

Do not goal set and leave it up to luck. He agreed with Vroom in that, first, followers make a calculating decision about their desired goals, identify the goals they intend to achieve, and then these goals and intentions direct or motivate their efforts to complete a task or attain the goals. Locke, probably, hinging upon David McClelland's work on motivation, argued, "Intentional behavior tends to keep going until it reaches completion." Most importantly, Locke helped leaders all over the world with his notion that goals that are consciously harder result in higher levels of performance. Just as a Karate expert improves punching speed by punching faster and more often, the human brain is programmed to work harder when pushed to do so. Coming from boot camp in the military or attempting to run a marathon will only prove this the case. Locke, ingeniously, coined this in his theory of goal setting. Prominent and standing the test of time, goal setting is the most powerful way to motivate your followers.

Locke provides characteristics of effective goals worth noting:

1) Challenging but realistic

2) Focused on a key result area

3) Linked to rewards

4) Accepted and endorsed

5) Related to a defined time frame

6) Specific and measurable

Building upon some of Vroom's work in motivation, Locke really places the emphasis on both the leader and follower---together, both can do amazing things.

Building on Locke's logic, SMART goals first appeared in the November 1981 issue of Management Review. "There's a S.M.A.R.T. way to write management goals and objectives." was the title and George Doran, Arthur Miller, and James Cunningham wrote it. This idea spread throughout both the academic and management-training scene quickly; not only in North America, but also throughout the world---- simple as it is!

Specific goals should be straightforward, specific in nature, and easy to accomplish. Here is where the action words such as direct, organize, coordinate, lead, develop, plan, and build may come into play.

Measurable goals are meant to establish concrete criteria for measuring progress toward the attainment of each goal you set. Being honest, however, goals may not be able to be accomplished overnight and may have to be broken down into smaller, more manageable goals to reach the end result.

Attainable goals are those that help you develop the right attitude, ability, skill level, and even the financial capacity to reach them. Michael Shayne Gary, Miles M. Yang, Philip W. Yetton, John D. Sterman, in 2017, introduced a compilation of "Stretch Goals and the Distribution of Organizational Performance." They published this in the Organization Science Journal. They argue that first, stretch goal advocates extend the generally accepted finding from the managerial psychology literature that challenging goals have a positive performance. While these scholars challenge stretch goals, "There is no empirical evidence or theoretical framework to support this generalization." In some cases, empirical evidence is not necessary or can easily be investigated. For the purposes of establishing attainable goals, set stretch goals to help you perform better at what you are trying to accomplish.

Realistic goals must be based on where you see yourself today now as a leader or where you determine your followers to be after examining and discussing their situations. You want to set the bar high enough so that you or your followers can satisfy achievement. Now this does not mean that if failure takes place that someone will be penalized. Failing will be discussed later, but for now, focus on setting realistic goals for you and your followers to build both performance and high self-esteem.

Time-Specific goals are placing an end point on your goal, which tends to give you a clear target to work toward. Without a time, limit, there is no urgency to start taking action.

Building a motivational mindset when deciding which goal to pursue and how to manage performance for that goal are some important points along with the others. Make sure, as a leader, your expectations are shared with the follower at the beginning of the performance period and then periodically revisited to ensure that the goals are being met. Remember that if you cannot describe expectations clearly then you cannot expect followers to achieve them. Also, giving positive feedback whenever possible is important. Intermittently rewarding performance can also be a great motivator.

The key point for leaders to consider is providing content theory to meet people's needs, if you are trying to sell something to followers, customers, or anyone for that matter. However, if you are in the office or in the field attempting to motivate followers, then use the process theory. There are two solid approaches:

1) Arouse a need for followers and then demonstrate a path toward that need via goal directed behavior so they can accomplish the task.

2) Arouse followers to do things for you using goal directed behavior to reach a desired outcome or goal. In organizational behavior, we have something called "shaping," in which we have a

final goal, which is built upon smaller goals that lead to the overall larger goal.

Ken Blanchard and Spencer Johnson wrote a book titled "The One Minute Manager" in 1982 with William Morrow and Company. It is a very short book that tells a story by recounting three techniques of an effective leader: one-minute goals, one-minute praises, and one-minute reprimands. With more than two million hardcover copies in print, The One Minute Manager ranks as one of the most successful management books ever published.

The book is about a young man who is in search of an effective manager and is willing to work for one when he finds him or her.

In the young man's search, he meets some 'autocratic' managers who are only concerned about the results. He also meets 'democratic' managers who are only concerned about the people. He was looking for an effective manager who was interested in the people as well as the results so that both the people and the organization could prosper. Interestingly enough, he hinged upon the leadership literature that was designed to look at leadership from a grid standpoint with people on one axis and the task on the other. This will be discussed later on in this book.

Then, the young man comes across a manager who calls himself "the one-minute manager". He claims to offer three secrets to the young man in his pursuit of learning how to become a manager. Ergo, the secrets:

FIRST SECRET: One-Minute Goals
One minute goal setting is about being aware of what is expected from the beginning, writing it down and pursuing it until it is completed and then deciding upon the next goal to pursue.

SECOND SECRET: One-Minute Praises
After the one-minute goal setting, the second step in one-minute management is to catch people doing something right. This is when the one-minute praises are given so that they have the best possible effect on followers. One-minute praises include praising the people immediately, telling them what they did right, how you feel about it and encouraging them to do more of the same.

THIRD SECRET: One-Minute Reprimands
One-minute reprimands are given as soon as an employee does something wrong. Again, to be most effective, reprimands need to be timely, accurate, and imparted on the correct follower(s).

Knowing Ken and Spencer's One Minute Management techniques and the three secrets will help leaders and their followers to become more motivated and perform at optimal levels.

When we think of motivating our followers, and ourselves we often feel how in control we are with ourselves. The same thing goes for your followers. The more controlled of themselves they feel, the more likely they are to succeed without a great deal of direction from you as their leader. Locus of control is something that each leader must be aware of and manage well.

Within psychology, Locus of Control is considered an important aspect of personality. Julian Rotter developed the concept originally in the 1950s. Locus of Control refers to an individual's perception about the underlying main causes of events in his or her life. These events transfer to the workplace when planning goals and objectives for both leaders and subordinates. How much internal control do you or your followers require?

If you have a high internal locus of control, you tend to have a great deal of free will and you feel in control of both your life and your actions in the workplace. You also take responsibility for both in that you try to make things happen for yourself as opposed to waiting for someone else to come along and open up some opportunity or project that may get you some exposure.

If you have a high external locus of control, you tend to defer to people of power and when you become in a higher leadership role, you expect others to defer to you. Interestingly enough, however, people with an external locus of control feel that they lack the ability to make choices and rely on the leader or government to support their ideas and accomplishments.

Another psychological type that adds to the motivational mindset is personality type.

Type A personality behavior was first described as a potential risk factor for heart disease in the 1950s by cardiologists Meyer Friedman and Ray Rosenman. Since then, academics and motivational gurus alike have used this idea to address motivation and personality. Your personality type has a lot to do with the way you view life. For instance, a Type A personality creates a behavior pattern that is labeled coronary-prone behavior. This is a complex personality with behavior characteristics that include competitiveness, time urgency, social status insecurity, aggression, hostility, and a quest for achievements. In addition, this personality type likes to be organized and keep things around them clean. Sound familiar?

The Type B behavior pattern is somewhat different in that people are less coronary prone. They take hassles less seriously and tend to find humor in situations.

Perhaps a good measure of a leader's character would be having both personality types (type A and type B) to ensure that they are both productive and happy. Finding joy in our work should be tantamount to our daily work experience. Is there a happy medium----a sweet spot---between the amount of work we do and the amount of free time we have with our loved ones, significant others, and spouses?

The three most common tools to motivate followers are money, of course, but also social recognition, a huge component in North America and other parts of the world, and performance feedback. Performance feedback is usually done yearly, and to suggest it to be done more often is a logistic nightmare for most leaders, but it still looms large as a potential common incentive and motivator.

"Pay well, pay fairly, and then do everything you can to get money off people's minds." -Alfie Kohn

"I find that the harder I work the more luck I seem to have." -Thomas Jefferson

Intrinsic motivation seems to be the key to all motivation and could be tantamount to a leader's reputation among followers. Intrinsic motivation is the inherent nature to seek out novelty and challenges. At some point in our career, for some the beginning, others the middle or end, we want to extend our capacity, perhaps explore new tasks and functions and learn or apply new things. A child may want recognition and the reward may be a nod or accolade. As adults we desire similar attention for our accomplishments.

We also have a natural inclination toward mastering what we do to the extent that we are able to do so.

Intrinsic motivation is essential to our lives and could be a principal source of enjoyment and objective throughout them.

All leaders should know the story of the Frog and the Scorpion. The origin of the fable is somewhat uncertain. One of the earliest known appearances of the fable is in the 1954 script of Orson Welles' film Mr. Arkadin.

The Scorpion and the Frog is an animal fable that seems to have first emerged in 1954. Because of its dark morality, there have been many references to it in popular culture since then, including in notable films, television shows, and books.

A scorpion asks a frog to carry it across a river. The frog hesitates, afraid of being stung, but the scorpion argues that if it did so, they would both drown. Considering this, the frog agrees, but midway across the river, the scorpion does indeed sting the frog, dooming them both. When the frog asks the scorpion why, the scorpion replies that it was in its nature to do so.

Leaders need to understand this story. There are all types of scorpions that we carry on our back. Some bite us do their inherent nature and some do so out of sheer ignorance or by not following correct procedure. Carelessness and ignorance are the nemeses of a great leader. However, the leader that can be proactive and take a bird's eye view of his followers will know when and where to interject his or her presence to swoop down and help them when necessary.

Jim Rohn, a guru in the motivational extent of literature, argues that leaders must also understand the story of shepherds, sheep, and wolves. Rohn makes an interesting analogy with what is said in the Bible. He says that there are shepherds and there are sheep and there are wolves, and therefore, you have to be careful because some wolves have learned and dress up like sheep. Wise leaders are aware of the wolves that disguise themselves as sheep and can point them out before they attempt to spread their natural tendencies to destroy a company's culture or do something unethical.

Direction, to be discussed later, is what people may need to accomplish their goal. A colleague of mine at the University of Wisconsin found that people have too many targets to select from when attempting to accomplish their goals. Therefore, the leader must help the follower select the right target to reach optimal productivity, such as the parable found in the Alice in Wonderland story with Alice and the Cheshire Cat:

"Alice: Would you tell me, please, which way I ought to go from here?
The Cheshire Cat: That depends a good deal on where you want to get to.
Alice: I don't much care where.
The Cheshire Cat: Then it doesn't much matter which way you go.
Alice: ...So long as I get somewhere.
The Cheshire Cat: Oh, you're sure to do that, if only you walk long enough." ___Lewis Carroll, Alice in Wonderland

We often look at success in a microcosm. What actually is your definition of success? A colleague of mine, Walter Einstein, in a doctoral seminar, mentioned that success is the progressive realization of worthwhile predetermined personal goals. It is progressive because it is about the journey rather than the destination, worthwhile because the intention is personal mastery or success of reaching your goals, and predetermined because the plan or goal puts you in the right direction. Jim Rohn once said, "Success, like luck, is the residual of design." Jim argued that if you set low goals you would end up achieving them but also end up holding yourself back and oppressing your true potential.

"Don't join an easy crowd; you won't grow. Go where the expectations

and the demands to perform are high." - Jim Rohn

    Do not compromise with what talents you have and sell yourself short. You want to achieve incremental improvement each day so that you keep growing and become what you were meant to be.
    Jim Rohn had one of the most powerful weekend seminars ever created. Some of the best motivational speakers came from his training to become prosperous---perhaps the great Tony Robbins was inspired by Jim's weekend seminar. Jim provides a great excerpt worth noting from his 2001 weekend event. For more information on this excellent motivational guru, go to jimrohn.com. Jim's words will follow below. Harness them.

Over the years as I've sought out ideas, principles and strategies to life's challenges, I've come across four simple words that can make living worthwhile.

First, life is worthwhile if you **LEARN**. What you don't know *WILL* hurt you. You have to have learning to exist, let alone succeed. Life is worthwhile if you learn from your own experiences—negative or positive. We learn to do it right by first sometimes doing it wrong. We call that a positive negative. We also learn from other people's experiences, both positive and negative....Learning from other people's experiences and mistakes is valuable information because we can learn what not to do without the pain of having tried and failed ourselves.

We learn by what we see, so pay attention. We learn by what we hear, so be a good listener. Now I do suggest that you should be a selective listener, don't just let anybody dump into your mental factory. We learn from what we read so learn from every source; learn from lectures; learn from songs; learn from sermons; learn from conversations with people who care. Always keep learning.

Second, life is worthwhile if you **TRY**. You can't just learn; now you have to try something to see if you can do it. Try to make a difference, try to make some progress, try to learn a new skill, try to learn a new sport. It doesn't mean you can do everything, but there are a lot of things you can do, if you just try. Try your best. Give it every effort. Why not go all out?

Third, life is worthwhile if you **STAY**. You have to stay from spring until harvest. If you have signed up for the day or for the game or for the project—see it through. Sometimes calamity comes and then it is worth wrapping it up. And that's the end, but just don't end in the middle. Maybe on the next project you pass, but on this one, if you signed up, see it through.

And **Lastly**, life is worthwhile if you **CARE**. If you care at all you will get some results, if you care enough you can get incredible results. Care enough to make a difference. Care enough to turn somebody around. Care enough to start a new enterprise. Care enough to change it all. Care enough to be the highest producer. Care enough to set some records. Care enough to win.

> Four powerful little words:
> **LEARN, TRY, STAY** and **CARE.**

> [Jim asks] What difference can you make in your life today by putting these words to work?

    We know now that goal setting is highly valued by both academics and scholars alike. The question we sometimes ask is, "How do we set goals?" Tony Robbins says to people, "This is who I am, and this is what I want to accomplish, and nothing will stop me from achieving my destiny." Self-talk like this is powerful. We often talk ourselves out of success. Tony offers a twelve-step process to goal setting:

- 1) Desire, 2) Belief, 3) Write it down, 4) List benefits, 5) Analyze your starting point, 6) Set a deadline, 7) Make a list of obstacles, 8) Identify additional information, 9) Make a list of people that will help you, 10) Make a plan, 11) Visualization, and 12) Never give up. Don't let anything stop you.

Set goals to mobilize your energy level and increase your effort. The key is to attempt to increase your persistence to achieve your goals. Randy Dunham, in his Management Workshop series, points out that motivation is a combination of intensity and direction; both are necessary to achieve your goals. He also points out that selecting the most appropriate tasks are very important.

Your belief system is also important. We often formulate a belief based on a fragment of the information available to us. Jim Rohn used to say, "What are you doing today?" He felt that you could choose some great things to accomplish for yourself each day or make a plan for the future to pursue your dreams. Many motivational speakers, including myself, have told people that they do not ever have to be the same after today----only by their own personal choice.

Your goal needs to be a servant leader, one who helps people with improving themselves. While it all begins with us, as we improve, we can pay it backward and forward. Pay back the people that helped, pay the people that need your help, and do not forget to pay yourself for all that you accomplish.

We see today from the tragic events around the world, and sometimes close to our home, what happens when you are not having fun and living in a high stress environment. Only you know how that feels and only you can make that change for yourself. First, knowing that you need help to change is necessary before it can happen. No one can tell you that you need help. They can suggest it, but only you will know when it is necessary to seek help or not.

Another key to motivation today is managing people during a crisis. When a crisis takes place, attempt to help people cope by being a role model for them to follow. Leaders should build empathy by attempting to see the situation from the person most affected by the situation and attempt to discuss it with them. A great leader once told me that when someone is upset and crying, if you ask him or her a question, they have to stop crying for a moment to answer it. This is a great technique and is valuable to know when you need to apply it after a crisis.

Positive psychology is important when a crisis arises because people tend to only focus on the negatives. Leaders need to push followers to think positively. The key is to get people to move forward in a small, but productive way. Even the slightest productivity alleviates anxiety.

Try to keep followers focused by moving away from the problem and focusing on the solutions. Finally, set a path for them to follow. Show appreciation when there is incremental improvement. Reward that behavior in some way and encourage more to continue that type of performance.

CONCLUSION

KEY TAKEAWAYS

1. Motivating people is more of an art than a science. If you have people, where you want them to be or even better, if they are where they want to choose to be, you have accomplished true motivation and will reap the benefits of loyalty and commitment. People will also be engaged, innovative, and creative.

Here are five ways to keep employees engaged:

a. Praise people in public and give them the necessary

podium-time to express their great ideas and/or accomplishments.

b. Let people be authentic in that they know their own personal strengths and weaknesses — build strengths and cross out weaknesses — let them succeed.

c. Remember where people came from — the pedigree personality has been replaced by hard work and assertiveness.

d. Take care of your people and they will join the culture, stick by the mission and vision, and be devoted.

e. Forget hourly pay — it is the most demeaning way to manage — let people work as many hours as they want as long as the work and the customers' are being serviced accordingly. Sure, people need to have a set wage and timeframe, but minimum wage is a starting point and not a platform for a status-quo career.

2. Lead from the front. Leaders that go out and engage with people are more appreciated and better equipped to succeed.

3. Develop a motivational plan for yourself that gets you doing what you love and as often as you can do it. The key here is that doing what you do on-the-job is important, but if you are in a dead-end career, then work is a means to engage in what you do outside of work for entertainment---a hobby, sports, vacations, etc.

4. Remember the people around you. You cannot motivate them, but you can express how their motivation affects you. This may or may not motivate them, but you will at least assert yourself and hopefully sleep better at night. Be self-aware and think about your authentic self as often as possible.

4

Pillar Four –
Managing People

"People who produce good results feel good about themselves." -Ken Blanchard

Managing people is the forefront of the four functions of management as mentioned earlier: controlling, leading, organizing, and planning. While all of these functions fall under management, they have their own important component that encompass the discipline of leadership. While leadership falls under the auspice of management, it has risen to a level that has developed into its own area and discipline among both academics and leadership experts in the workplace.

- Planning is setting and attaining goals. You have planned well your entire life but the focus here is on conscious and proactive planning. When having to be reactive, a plan to follow has already been set

in place and can be altered to address a new issue as it arises.
- Organizing pertains to ascertaining human and physical resources to get the job done. Leaders must be very organized, or they may fail. Some leaders have excellent administrative assistants and other valuable human assets and systems to help them succeed in organization.
- Leading encompasses every chapter of this book and pertains to achieving organizational objectives. While being only a component of the four functions of management, leading makes astute leaders realize that the four functions are only a part of their day-to-day operation.

Henri Fayol, a scholar from France, came up with the functions of management. Known as Jules Henri Fayol, his experience was the Managing Director in business. He viewed management as the general activity of integrating functions of the firm in order to intelligently use resources to attain the objectives of the firm. According to Dan Wren and Arthur Bedian, two exceptional management history scholars, Fayol was at the heart of management as a process. Dan was a close colleague during my doctoral studies and encouraged me to write an article, which I titled similar to the title of his book, a true academic management historian that loves management history. Arthur was the first scholar to tell me to read everything, and he meant everything in your field of study. Therefore,

I touched just about every article ever written in management and leadership---and what he said became the best advice I ever received.

Here is an excerpt from their book titled "The Evolution of Management Thought," which is the premier book on management history. Fayol felt that every organization required management regardless of whether it was focused on commercial, industry, politics, religion, or war. These are his list of managerial qualities:

- **Physical qualities**: health, vigor, address
- **Mental qualities**: ability to understand and learn, judgment, mental vigor, and adaptability
- **Moral qualities**: energy, firmness, willingness to accept responsibility, initiative, loyalty, tact, dignity
- **General education**: general acquaintance with matters not belonging exclusively to the function performed
- **Special knowledge**: that peculiar to the function, be it technical, commercial, financial, managerial, etc.

◻ **Experience**: knowledge arising from the work proper; the recollection of lessons a person has derived from things

Leading is a function of management, but for the sake of this book, and to your success, Six Factor Leadership is really about putting everything you know to work to succeed. Take these qualities, build on them each day, each week, each month, each year, and watch your career prosper.

- Controlling ensures that performance conforms to plans. Some scholars talk about feedforward, feedback ward, and perhaps feed current for that matter. Marshall Goldsmith is an American leadership coach and the author of several management-related books. He is a big proponent of the "feedforward" idea. So is Professor Avraham Kluger, an organizational behavior expert, who writes: Unlike feedback, which has multiple detrimental consequences, feedforward creates positive emotions, fosters bonding, builds psychological safety, and promotes the elicitation and sharing of vital new information regarding keys for personal and organizational flourishing. Joel Trammell often posts great ideas like the one above that leaders can directly apply to their organization in his blog called "The Khoros Blog."

You, as an executive, plan the most while supervisors lead face-to-face the most. The technical workers are usually at the lower echelon of the organization. As Dan and Arthur capture in their book, Fayol really nailed it:

Managerial abilities become more important as a person moves up in the hierarchy. Technical abilities are less essential for upper-level managers.

This idea is not to place technological skill at a lower priority.

Technical skills may have helped you achieve the position that you have now, and those skills may be dear to you; use them coupled with your new skill of conceptual thinking as a leader and executive.

An important concept of managing people is a complete and thorough understanding of emotional intelligence. Daniel Goleman is an author and science journalist. For twelve years, he wrote for The New York Times, reporting on the brain and behavioral sciences. His work has reached across the spectrum of academia, leadership boardrooms, and management trainers across the globe.

The key to emotional intelligence is to show that you care about your followers, build trust, and show sensitivity to the issues facing the human resources that you manage. While your main goal is to motivate others, most importantly you must be able to motivate yourself to have enough energy to complete your day-to-day tasks while motivating yourself and others to continuously improve.

According to psychologist Daniel Goleman in his monumental book "Emotional Intelligence: Why It Can Matter More Than IQ," "emotional intelligence" (EQ) is another aspect of intelligence that is often overlooked by leaders in the workplace. Steven Handle captured this aspect of EQ well in his article "The Emotion Machine." Steve calls the components of EI "The 4 Fundamental Pillars of Emotional Intelligence."

Goleman has noted some ideas from past notaries and authorities of thinking and Steve captured that here:

In light of his theory of evolution, Charles Darwin theorized that our minds have evolved to experience emotions so that we can better adapt to our environment.

Let us look at Steve's view of emotional intelligence and the four pillars:

- **Self-Awareness:** The first pillar of emotional intelligence is paying attention to your own emotions. Emotions often come in two main parts: 1) *The psychological component* – the thoughts, attitudes, and beliefs that underlie most of our emotions, and 2) *The physical component* – the bodily sensations that often accompany different emotional states.
- **Self-Regulation:** Once you are more aware of your emotions, the next pillar of emotional intelligence is learning how to respond to them better. An example is by channeling an emotion in a new and constructive way, such as through exercising, writing, or painting. Some more examples are avoiding triggers that are more likely to bring out a negative emotion, seeking positive experiences to reverse negative ruts, and turning emotions around by doing the opposite of what you feel; sitting and watching emotions as a passive observer instead of acting on them impulsively.
- **Empathy:** Understanding your own emotions is half of emotional intelligence; the other half is understanding the emotions of others.

- **Social Skills:** Once you understand the emotions of yourself and others, the next question is "How do I respond to other people's emotions?" This is where social skills come in as the last pillar of emotional intelligence.

Goleman built upon Howard Gardner's work in the area of multiple intelligence. Dr. Howard Gardner, professor of education at Harvard University, developed the theory of multiple intelligences in 1983. It suggests that the traditional notion of intelligence, based on I.Q. testing, is far too limited. Instead, Dr. Gardner proposes eight different intelligences to account for a broader range of human potential in children and adults. While Gardner introduced a great deal of awareness away from intelligence quotient, he failed to draw a great deal of attention in the extant literature. Goleman nailed it!

Leaders must be aware of organizational limitations while adapting to work with the system and culture in which they spend their work life.

Managing emotions in the workplace has become a major problem in some organizations and there are often limited or no consequences for bad behavior. Dysfunctional organizations tolerate emotional outbursts in some industries and the workplace become a hostile environment. To offset this dysfunctional work environment, executives have come up with a "No Jerk" policy.

Lisa O'Carroll, a reporter in December of 2011, published an article titled "***Barclay's boss reveals the 'No Jerks' rule***" in ***The Guardian*** news. Companies all over America joined the cause to enforce the no-jerk policy.

This was the second big Human Relations movement; only to the Hawthorne Effect by Elton Mayo and Harvard researchers decades earlier. The **Hawthorne Effect** is the inclination of people who are the subjects of an experimental study to change or improve the behavior being evaluated only because it is being studied and not because of changes in the experiment parameters or stimulus (Reviewed by INVESTOPEDIA Staff and updated on April 10, 2018). People felt loved and appreciated just by participating in the experiment and this set off a new dimension of caring about people and showing them appreciation. Productivity went up and the study revealed that human resources are valuable assets in the workplace.

Bob Diamond said "jerk" bankers were epitomized by an infamous 2002 episode in which six of Barclay's staff ran up a £44,000 alcohol tab over lunch at a London restaurant.

Bob Diamond says he has kicked out 30 of his staff for breaking his new ethics rule and warns that 'no one should ever not be nice.' Other leaders have found that people that learn to agree with others, in some way, or agree to disagree, is a good personality characteristic. For example, Hackman and Oldman in 1975 created a *Development of the Job Diagnostic Survey* and published it in the Journal of Applied Psychology. These management scholars note that "Agreeableness" is highly rated as a motivational aspect of an exceptional follower. On the other hand, another executive found that the 'No Jerk' policy struck a chord as he found that more people desired to work at a place where they are treated like people and not just human resources.

George Sims, McLean, and Mayer wrote an article in 2007 titled "Discovering Your Authentic Leadership" in the Harvard Business Review. These scholars found that 75 members of Stanford Graduate School of Business's Advisory Council were asked to recommend the most important capability for leaders to develop, their answer was nearly unanimous: ***self-awareness.***

The key is to be an authentic leader. By knowing their authentic selves requires the courage and honesty to open up and examine their experiences and by doing this, leaders become more humane and willing to be vulnerable. The key is to practice the habit of not having to be right all the time and seek out people to help when necessary; even a "No" person on occasion.

The brain is an amazing organ and has capabilities that go far beyond our own belief system. Research on the brain has led to an understanding that each of us have a preferred way and mode of thinking that affects the way we take in and process information. The awareness of one's own thinking preferences and the thinking preferences of others combined with the ability to act outside of one's preferred thinking preferences is known as "Whole Brain® Thinking." Many people look at the brain as both intuitive and logical. However, some people feel that they may be both good at mathematical equations and that they are still intuitive. Herrmann came up with four quadrants. For example, upper left quadrant is for analytical reasoning while lower left is for sequential thinking. Upper right thinking is more intuitive while the lower right is emotional.

Another colleague of mine that I aspire to often is Richard Felder (with Barbara Soloman; both scholars are well known and reside at North Carolina State University) with his research titled *"LEARNING STYLES AND STRATEGIES."* I strongly advise you to google it, take the 44-question survey, and see your results immediately. I use this when I train executives in both leadership and technical writing. The one style I like to address often is Global versus Sequential. This one quadrant can make or break a leader/follower relationship.

Leaders are aware of the Self-Fulfilling Prophecy that recognizes that what we believe to be true usually formulates into reality for us in some way. Therefore, how we think things are - what we think is true - what we expect, as a likely consequence that will follow from our behavior is also likely to manifest itself in our day-to-day lives. At work, if we plan to move up the ladder and communicate that well to our leaders, we tend to thrive. In some cases, there is not enough room for leaders, and then we focus on staying a follower---but at this level, there are many opportunities to lead.

What we create through our thoughts is a belief system and that ultimately determines success in life.

Lenchioni recalls the most transparent and well-known catastrophe in the corporate boardroom in his article titled *"Make Your Values Mean Something"* in the

Harvard Business Review. Here is an excerpt from Lenchioni:

"Take a look at this list of corporate values: Communication. Respect. Integrity. Excellence. They sound pretty good, don't they? Strong, concise, meaningful. Maybe they even resemble your own company's values, the ones you spent so much time writing, debating, and revising. If so, you should be nervous. These are the corporate values of Enron, as stated in the company's 2000 annual report. And as events have shown, they're not meaningful; they're meaningless."

Leaders should be aware of the brain's capacity to store and retrieve messages that influence their daily decision making and thought process. The limbic system helps us know what things to approach and what to avoid – strong intuition and gut feeling because our limbic system has more information stored over time. Experience builds a knowledge base that is the best. Many leaders are not conscious about the limbic part of the brain. It is where all of your beliefs and habits from our childhood and adulthood are stored. The limbic system controls how we feel and how we feel influences our behavior to act. We become more motivated to act and our thinking, and with all of our experience, learning is enhanced over time. I often tell people that each day, each hour, and each minute, we are changing and growing and how we think at the end of the day could be radically different from when we woke up this morning. An interesting thing is that the limbic system also simply interprets sensory information and dispatches it to another part of the brain called the cortex.

The cortex is a part of the brain that we are in-tune with. This part of the brain is a region that is indicative of planning complex cognitive behaviors. This is where we develop our personality, our expression, and our decision-making is made in a conscious way based on this region of the brain. Even social behavior is moderated by the way we act due to the cortex. The cortex is a conscious center of the brain that hears what you are thinking and can intellectually control behavior for processing, and we can also feel in control due to the knowledge and experience of which we are consciously aware. Therefore, we can orchestrate thoughts and actions in accordance with the internal goals we set. The limbic sets the emotional tone of the information before it reaches the cortex. Once stored in the brain, the cortex allows us to focus on emotional triggers to influence our behavior. Stephen Synek on social media captured this well as he looked at why leaders succeed at what they do. We sometimes do not realize the experience and knowledge that we manifest throughout our life from childhood, through adulthood, and most importantly, in the workplace. You have what it takes to lead. All you have to do is believe it and let your Limbic and Cortex lead the way for you.

The cortex can offer constructive rational beliefs if that is how you are wired. In order to be positive, constructive, and adaptive, you will have to try to stay in the moment. It is easy to dwell on the past and focus on the future, but your real strength as a leader is to focus on the present every moment of every day. You cannot control what another person says or does, but you can control your thoughts about it and how you react to it. Our thoughts play an important role in how we learn to control our emotions and our behavior. Jack Canfield, star of "The KEEPER of the KEYS", explains how we have the power to change the OUTCOMES in our lives by changing our RESPONSE to the events in our lives. Fabulous method for improving your life! Jack's formula:

Jack Canfield: E + R = O

People have events that happen in their life and then they add their response, and both added together equal the outcome. Many people look at the outcome and then they create a response to that outcome. When we change our response and the way we think about the outcome, then we can manage others and ourselves better. Destructive irrational beliefs according to Dr. Ellis in his work titled "How to Control Your Anger Before it Controls You" lead to negative emotions like anxiety, anger, and depression. Instead, Ellis argues that you should consider:

1) The best course of action
2) Look at all your options first
3) Make the best decision and then act upon it!

Basically, as a leader in charge of not only your own reactions to events but also other people's reaction to events, you must change your **feelings,** change your **behaviors,** and most importantly, to be effective, **change your beliefs.**

The key to your success is found in the bible verse from the Ecclesiastes (9:10) NIV, which states that:

WHAT EVER YOUR HAND(S) FIND TO DO, DO IT WITH ALL YOUR MIGHT!

Motivation comes from within; as Janet Provitera once said, "Motivation is the music inside of you." The reason why motivation is an internal force is that it drives individuals to act or achieve a specific goal. For instance, two people listen to the same inspirational audio and one person is motivated to act, while the other is not.

We often wonder why people are not like us or that they may not be as motivated as we are. The answer is simple. Motivation cannot be controlled by someone other than ourselves; when a leader is coercive, it usually is not genuine and does not last long even if the task is accomplished correct and/or on time. In a motivational video created by the author for the Mastering Self-Motivation book, one line in the video that people tend to remember is to avoid toxic people. Toxic people are not motivated the way we would like them to be, but they sure can be motivated to remain toxic. Our goal as leaders is to attempt to assert ourselves if possible and try not to become toxic ourselves, but at the same time respect the leader and support them. Even as a leader, we may have to deal with toxic people and this reality we have to face head on and cannot shy away from. The key is to think positive---and if the toxic person is our leader, we do not cause conflict in our relationship while we remain calm, cool, and collected.

Too many people are *NOT* 100% committed to working at peak performance and every day business suffers for one reason or another. It is leadership's responsibility to fix this problem. As Blake and Mouton, the authors of "Managerial Grid: Leadership Styles for Achieving Production through People," published in 1966, once mentioned that many people are at the "Middle of the Road." This connotation indicated that they were average when it comes to concern for production and people. This profound book in organizational development began the framework for many leadership models used by executives today. Thus, The Managerial Grid has caused leaders to not only believe that their goal for both high profitability and success is imminent, but also encouraged them to conduct their leadership role with style and pizzazz. In the article "Managerial Grid by Blake and Mouton" by P. Mulder in 2012 found at Toolshero dot com, Mulder realized that the Grid was the precursor to the Situational Leadership Model by Paul Hersey.

> **Anticipating on situational leadership, American Robert Blake and Jane Mouton arrived at the conclusion in 1964 that the behavior of a leader stems from two criteria: people orientation (concern for people) and task orientation (concern for production). In the so-called managerial grid, they combined these two criteria as a result in which a grid with 81 leadership styles was created.___P. Mulder**

Mulder (2012) presents an excellent comparison of the middle-of-the-road leader and the team-management leader. See P. Mulder's rendition of the Grid's 5.5 and 9.9 below.

5.5 Middle of the road

In this leadership style, the 'happy medium' course is adopted. The leader maintains a balance between the needs of the people and the production and the leader scores an average mark on both criteria. According to Robert Blake and Jane Mouton this is not always an ideal leadership style but because of pressure of time such as meeting deadlines, it is a good way to encourage the employees.

9.9 Team Management

The leader that is oriented towards this style should not change this. His employees form a close-knit team and work together on the execution of objectives. The leader has a lot of respect for his employees, provides enthusiasm, and motivates them. This is why they are able to bring out the best in themselves, Mutual involvement among the employees is high and they are very loyal to their employer. Such an optimal cooperation is often linked to short-term projects that are carried out by (highly) experienced employees. By paying a lot of attention to the needs of the employees and the production this leader works very efficiently.

Which leader are you? A middle-of-the-road leader or a team-management leader? While this is a rhetorical question, ask yourself the question:

"What is the most important thing you can do with your clients, followers or subordinates?"

The answer is undoubtedly to:

"INFLUENCE THEIR BEHAVIOR"

Authors have agreed with this philosophy of leadership. Just ask Cuddy, Khout, and Neffinger, who argue that to exert influence, you must balance competence with warmth. In their article with Harvard Business Review in 2013, like their title, they feel that leaders should "Connect, then Lead!"

Niccolò Machiavelli, the author of the classic book titled "The Prince" written in 1532, asked the question, "Is it better to be loved or feared?" Be careful before you answer that question because depending on your experience and your industry, you may be wrong.

Sherill Hartzel, an author and professor at study.com argues that manipulation can be a powerful tool that is frequently put into practice by people who have a Machiavellian personality. Machiavellianism, often abbreviated as "Mach," is a personality trait that is characterized with the use of manipulation to achieve power. In her online lesson, she describes characteristics of Machiavellianism in both high and low Machs. This is nothing new, but her take on it is very enlightening. Let me provide you with an excerpt from her lesson:

According to Hartzel, psychologists have developed a series of instruments called Mach scales to measure a person's Machiavellian orientation. The continuum spans from being highly manipulative to being highly submissive. High Machs are those who would be considered highly manipulative, not easily persuaded, but persuade others more than low Machs. These leaders are successful in reaching their goals and tend to win more. People with a high Mach personality tend to be calm, unattached, calculated and look for ways to exploit loose structures or vulnerability in people. High Machs flourish in face-to-face settings where there are limited rules and structure and when emotions hold little value in goal achievement. Therefore, high Machs are best matched in professions that reward their 'do whatever it takes' attitude such as sales or jobs that offer commission for results.

Low Machs are on the opposite side of the Mach spectrum and are characterized as being highly submissive. Those individuals with a low Mach orientation are willing to accept direction imposed on them and thrive in highly structured situations. Low Machs are less motivated by things such as power, status, money and competition than high Machs are. Winning is not everything for low Machs; they operate with a much higher set of ethical standards than their high Mach counterparts.

According to Dr. Sherell Hartzel, Machiavellianism can be both positive and negative in organizations depending on how it is used. When Machiavellianism is used to increase managerial effectiveness by providing necessary direction to subordinates to accomplish organizational goals, it is considered a positive attribute. However, when Machiavellianism is used for personal gain at the expense of subordinate or organizational success, it would be considered highly negative.

Think of your status in your organization and the people that you lead. Are you a high or low Mach? Is a high Mach rewarded or shunned upon at your organization? Perhaps there are times when being a high Mach is necessary. Remember, knowledge is power and Niccovelli realized this in the 15th century so keep on learning and developing yourself and the followers that need your leadership. Machiavellianism has stood the test of time; look at your work environment and see how it fits and review your psychological aspect of status on the high Mach to low Mach.

Returning to Cuddy, Kohut, and Neffinger's article "Connect, then Lead," the authors argue that leaders should project warmth and strength. Warmth can be enhanced with delight rather than obsequious flattery or excessive admiration or praise. Always attempt to validate feelings. The authors state that as a leader, you should first agree with people in some way, shape, or form before you get them to listen and agree with you. Most importantly, smile and mean it. This could be not only self-reinforcing but also contagious.

Strength, on the other hand, according to Cuddy, Kohut, and Neffinger, is much more disciplined and detailed. These three things, if used accordingly, can develop into characteristics and traits:

- **Feel in command** – warmth may be harder to fake, but confidence is harder to talk yourself into. Avoid self-doubt.
- **Stand up straight** – good posture projects authority, regardless of your height.
- **Get a hold of yourself** – Move deliberately and precisely. Stillness demonstrates calm. Combine that with good posture, and you will achieve what is known as poise

telegraphing equilibrium and stability, important aspects of credible leadership presence.

Sometimes simple things such as the three insights above could make or break a personality, leadership, career, and help promo ability within any organization. Ronald Reagan, American politician and actor who served as the 40th President of the United States from 1981 to 1989, stood directly straight with a balance on both legs and only moved when he felt that he wanted to drive a point. Picture yourself leaning on a podium and then get a sense of what that looks like to your followers; probably not a good stance for a presentation and indicative of a lack of energy. Stand erect and convey purpose in your body structure. Also, at times, and especially when delegating, lean in when directing your group. Never look at your watch---this mistake added to the loss of a debate between Senior Bush United States Presidential incumbent and opponent Bill Clinton. In a U.S. News and World report article, this was coined as a triumph win for Clinton. The mistake of looking at the watch was the telltale sign of a man made uneasy—or, at least, bored—by an audience member's question about how a deep recession had personally affected him. The then president's display of impatience seemed to speak volumes more than his awkward response. His action was labeled as a damaging impatience.

In 2002, an article conducted a study that found optimists report a higher quality of life than pessimists do therefore, pessimists may pose health risks. The Mayo Clinic study found that pessimists had a 19 percent increase in death rate over optimists. Therefore, Positive

Thinking reduces tension and enhances emotional well-being and cardiovascular health, helps us to be more resilient in the face of difficulties, causes us to have healthier lifestyle habits, and helps us cope with stress more easily.

Earl Nightingale came up with the most powerful analogy in his piece called "The Strangest Secret," in which he determines the power of planning the right seed as a goal. Earl Nightingale was an American radio speaker and author, dealing mostly with the subjects of human character development, motivation, and meaningful existence; setting the standard of success for motivational gurus today. He said that the "Law of Attraction is considered by many to be the most important law of all in explaining both success and failure." If you plant a seed that is good and give it sun and water, it will grow but he argues that people can plant the wrong seeds and they will grow too. This may be the cause of corruption, the easy way out, gangs, and violence. Most importantly, mediocre performance that is enhanced by a weak goal or tacit thoughts that lead to limitations and oppression, and in some cases, depression.

"*Whatever we think about, we bring about.*" - *Earl Nightingale*

A good example of this is the balloon exercise that becomes a literal connection between what we want and the obstacles we face when we set goals. A simple exercise that places goals on a balloon of choice while others are fictitious but could be in the way of an original goal selected by the person tapping the balloons. We must be laser focused and take the time out to ensure that we reach our goals and become as successful as we wish to be. We must learn to manage ourselves first, and then take the time to manage others. Create a template for achieving your life and work goals with action steps, follow-up, and feedback. Establish rapport with your followers by:

- Building better relationships
- Continuous improvement
- Individual attention
- Modeling communication styles to followers
- Develop effective relationships
- Treat each person based on their situation (Tony Allessandra calls this the Platinum Rule as opposed to the Golden Rule)
- Always be truthful to establish trust

Remember your non-verbal as well as your verbal communication. Non-verbal accounts for much more than words do. Get in sync with the person or people whom you are interacting. Mihaly Csikzentmihalyi calls this "FLOW." When we are in sync, we communicate a level of understanding and empathy with people at their level at that particular time.

Being emotionally intelligent also includes being politically savvy. Having empathy, managing our emotions, and using effective communication techniques help enhance how positively we are perceived by our followers, colleagues, and superiors. Always remain objective and do not get drawn into the emotional frenzy that can surround unpopular decision-making. Attempt to remain logical and objective and stay away from water-cooler discussions and socializing outside of work.

Develop an astute political awareness. Just as authentic leaders attempt to discover their uniqueness, all leaders must be aware of their political attributes. Accurately read key power relationships, secure friendships and allies early on in your career, and maintain them. Networking is an ongoing process. This will give you the exposure necessary to develop insight into your career. External realities may become local issues and affect your leadership prowess as you manage in a world that is constantly changing and in flux.

Great leaders look among their followers to determine who can be an informal leader. Look for informal leaders that may wield influence among your staff, clients, customers, or group members. Give them the attention they desire and attempt to get your followers to respect them to a certain extent---even without formal titles. These types of relationships will build teams, which is another component of Emotional Intelligence. Teams are the foundation of an organization's success or failure, and they rely on relationship building. Good relationships among teams are dependent upon the strength of the emotional intelligence utilized by the team. Learn to be a coach, mentor, and facilitator. Al Pacino said it best in the movie "Any Given Sunday."

If we cannot work as a team, we will fail as individuals! -Al Pacino, "Any Given Sunday" movie

All leaders can derive lessons from geese. Dr. Robert McNeish of Baltimore wrote lessons from the Geese in 1972. Dr. McNeish was for many years a science teacher before he became involved in school administration. He had been intrigued by geese and observed them for years; writing the piece for a sermon, he delivered in his church. This sermon has taken on a new meaning for leaders and has inspired many people. Here is a version of his excellent research in this area:

Lesson 1 - The Importance of Achieving Goals

As each goose flaps its wings, it creates an UPLIFT for the birds that follow. By flying in a 'V' formation, the whole flock adds 71 percent extra to the flying range.

Outcome

When we have a sense of community and focus, we create trust and can help each other to achieve our goals.

Lesson 2 - The Importance of Team Work

When a goose falls out of formation, it suddenly feels the drag and resistance of flying alone. It quickly moves back to take advantage of the lifting power of the birds in front.

Outcome

If we had as much sense as geese, we would stay in formation with those headed where we want to go. We are willing to accept their help and give our help to others.

Lesson 3 - The Importance of Sharing

When a goose tires of flying, up front, it drops back into formation and another goose flies to the point position.

Outcome

It pays to take turns doing the hard tasks. We should respect and protect each other's unique arrangement of skills, capabilities, talents and resources.

Lesson 4 - The Importance of Empathy and Understanding

When a goose gets sick, two geese drop out of formation and follow it down to the ground to help and protect it.

Outcome

If we have as much sense as geese we will stand by each other in difficult times, as well as when we are strong.

Lesson 5 - The Importance of Encouragement

Geese flying in formation 'HONK' to encourage those up front to keep up with their speed.

Outcome

We need to make sure our honking is encouraging. In groups and teams where there is encouragement, production is much greater. 'Individual empowerment results from quality honking'

By far, one of the best well-known leaders that we can learn from in the corporate sector is Jack Welch. His wealth of knowledge cannot be captured in a paragraph. However, here are ten career busters to avoid:

1-Misfiring on performance or values—Overcommitting and under-delivering.

2-Resistance to change—Failing to embrace new ideas.

3-Being a Problem Identifier vs. a Problem Solver.

4-Winning over your boss but not your business peer group.

5-Always worrying about your next career move versus focusing on the present.

6-Running for office—it's totally transparent to everyone but you!

7-Self-importance—exhibiting a humorless, rigid attitude.

8-Lacking the courage and conviction to push back on the system.

9-Forgetting to develop your own succession plan for when you get promoted.

10-Complacency—you've stopped growing.

In summary, when managing people, employ all your emotional competencies to your relationships---self-awareness, self-regulation, self-motivation, and empathy---to influence and persuade others. Build consensus and support for team goals, and most importantly, as Dan

Goleman says, motivate and inspire yourself and others to achieve those goals. Goffee and Jones in their Harvard Business Review article titled "Why Should Anyone Be Led by You," offers the SO-WHAT that many academics and business leaders look for when applying leadership techniques, ideas, models, and even theory. These authors, Goffee and Jones, discovered that inspirational leaders also share four unexpected qualities:

- Humanity---By exposing some vulnerability, they reveal their approachability
- Act---Their ability to collect and interpret soft data helps them know just when and how to get in touch with people
- Do----Inspirational leaders empathize passionately—and realistically—with people, and they care intensely about the work that employees engage in.
- Themselves----They capitalize on what's unique about themselves instead of comparing to others.

There are three ancient yet still-used persuasive appeals. The first one, Ethos, an ethical appeal, is used to show an audience that you are a credible source who is worth listening to. Second, Pathos, an emotional appeal, is used to get the audience to feel what you want them to feel, and the third, Logos, a logical appeal, is used to convince the audience that you are logical, and your message is well reasoned. Seek progress, not perfection; most importantly, enjoy the journey, you only get one chance at life----live it!

Conclusion

There are four functions of management as mentioned earlier – controlling, leading, organizing, and planning. While leadership falls under the auspice of management, it has risen to a level that has developed into its own area and discipline among both academics and leadership experts in the workplace.

KEY TAKEAWAYS

1. Managing people is not as easy as it appears to be. Ben Franklin, one of the founding fathers of America, developed four management lessons, which is published by Glenn, in 2016, on quickbase dot com.

    a. Diligence is the mother of good luck – work hard on yourself and develop you talent to the best of your ability.

b. Wise men learn by others' harms, fools by their own - the Bible, the Tora, the Koran, or many other versions of biblical scholarship are based on half of what to do right and the other half of what to avoid or not do wrong.

c. Beware of little expenses; a small leak will sink a great ship – We often live in a paperless society when it comes to currency, and we hope to use plastic and online credit accounts to buy things as if our money grows on trees. We must find a budget, some semblance of management of our money to reap the benefits of business and personal growth.

d. Speak little, do much – Let your actions tell your story instead of your story telling about your actions. Let others determine your success, if you are success, someone will boast about your progress. Accept it humbly. As Glenn states "Ben Franklin would be proud."

2. Watch out for people who are dissatisfied with their work or personal life, they may try to sabotage you.
3. Remember to always manage yourself before you attempt to either manage up or down. People watch you and mirror your actions. Use the four functions of management and watch people follow your lead. The four functions of management are (CLOP) ---- Control, Lead, Organize, and Plan.
4. Change is something that we will always face. We may not want to face the change in front of us, but in some

cases, there is nothing we can do about it. In the book "Who Moved My Cheese" by Spencer Johnson, the author helps us deal with the inevitable change that we will continuously face. However, Carmen Nobel, in September 2011, wrote an article titled "Cheese Moving: Effecting Change Rather Than Accepting It." Nobel states, "With more than 23 million copies in print, Spencer Johnson's allegorical tale 'Who Moved My Cheese?' is one of the best-selling business books of all time. Even 13 years after its initial publication, the book, whose characters include mice in a maze, still sits at the top of Amazon.com's Workplace Behavior best-seller list—thanks in part to corporate managers who distribute it to their employees as a lesson in accepting and anticipating change gracefully. But is that really the best message to send?" Malhotra disagrees.

"In my view, we should really think twice before telling would-be innovators, problem solvers, and leaders that instead of wasting their time wondering why things are the way they are, they should simply accept their world as given." - Deepak Malhotra

"I Moved Your Cheese *is based on the idea that success in the areas of innovation, entrepreneurship, creativity, leadership, and business growth—as well*

as personal growth—depends on the ability to push the boundaries, reshape the environment, and play by a different set of rules—our own," says *Malhotra*.

5

Pillar Five – Core Leadership Principles

"People who produce good results feel good about Themselves." -Ken Blanchard

    This chapter covers some leadership models that I use in training executives. There is a plethora of leadership material that managers can embrace. My goal is to bring out the best of leadership and deliver it in a format that is easily digested and applied. Since this whole book is based on the concept of leadership, one would entertain the fact of how a chapter could be dedicated to the subject. The reason is that leadership is much more than just the encapsulation of a word; it is a process and a mechanism that is unique to each individual. Two people can lead in a great way but can have very different ways of doing so. Sit back and enjoy the chapter----I assure you that it will take on a new form of interest that perhaps you have been already exposed to but could use a refresher on.

Although leadership can encompass many forms, styles, and models, I have found over the last twenty years of training executives that focusing on one style and mastering it provides a better leader-follower relationship. Knowing a second or third model of leadership is also a good attribute, but the focus has been on leading and not trying to compartmentalize knowledge into a box that is closed. Step outside of the box and expand your comfort zone to encourage followers through inspiration, hard work, and laser focus.

Here is a book all leaders should read that brings out the most important aspects of leadership. My first choice is Harvard Business School of Business – read this excerpt of topics and then contemplate how you can expand on your leadership competencies:

As Al Deming once said in his 14 points of Total Quality Management, Continue learning. Here is a book to consider for your leadership library. It includes 17 skills that leader's should possess. Published by Harvard Business Review on January 3, 2017. A must read for executives and aspiring leaders. Here is a description provided by Harvard Business Review (all rights reserved for HBR):

The one primer you need to develop your managerial and leadership skills. Whether you're a new manager or looking to have more influence in your current management role, the challenges you face come in all shapes and sizes--a direct report's anxious questions, your boss's last-minute assignment of an important presentation, or a blank business case staring you in the face. To reach your full potential in these situations, you need to master a new set of business and personal skills. Packed with step-by-step advice and wisdom from "Harvard Business Review's" management archive, the "HBR Manager's Handbook" provides best practices on topics from understanding key financial statements and the fundamentals of strategy to emotional intelligence and building your employees' trust. The book's brief sections allow you to home in quickly on the solutions you need right away--or take a deeper dive if you need more context. Keep this comprehensive guide with you throughout your career and be a more impactful leader in your organization. Transition to Leadership.

Build trust and credibility
Emotional intelligence
Positioning yourself for success
Become a person of influence
Communicating effectively
Personal productivity
Self-development
Delegating with confidence
Giving effective feedback
Developing talent
Leading Teams
Fostering creativity
Hiring and keeping
Strategy: A Primer
Mastering Financial Tools
Developing a Business Case Study

Core Leadership Principles

Simon Sinek on the social media circuit has established a great rapport with his famous speech on knowing the "Why" of leadership. He states in his video and other social media that people buy ideas from leaders because of what is in it for them and not because they have to or even need to. The trust-building aspect of business is interesting and too often overlooked – Are you sharing your "why" with constituents and followers? How might you be more successful if you do? Sinek answers these questions by using ideas from the Wright brothers in flight and Martin Luther King in his work titled "How Great Leaders Inspire Action."

The first thing a leader must understand before requiring followers to take on a task is if they are directing correctly. Once you train someone else to take over one of your tasks, you will be freed up to move on to new, more strategic endeavors. However, many leaders hold onto tasks for multiple reasons. One of those reasons is a lack of trust – and trust is key to success. What is keeping you from delegating to some employees but not others? In addition, most importantly, how can you fix this problem?

The best way is to select the best delegate for the job. Consider how independent the person is, what he/she wants from the job, what his/her long-term goals and interests are and how they align with the proposed assignment, whether or not they are available to take on more, or not. Matching the task to the ability will provide a better outcome. Do not just dump a project on someone: engage him or her in the process, reward him or her, and do not criticize him or her. Your goal is to get your followers to feel the same way you do about the task. The key to leadership is also to remember that your followers may be better at a task then you are and that is perfectly acceptable.

Delegation will free you up for the more conceptual ideas and concerns that you face. You can delegate to improve follower motivation, morale, manage the day-to-day workload more effectively. This gives followers a sense of ownership and empowerment. Effective leaders do not give up their lives for their jobs; they delegate well and free themselves up for things that are more important. Your goal to accomplish is, "How can you empower people to complete the task on their own without your help?"

Kurt Lewin developed leadership style in the 1930s. Many subsequent leadership styles are based on his original work. He looked at the authoritative versus the autocratic leader, free rein versus laissez-faire leaders, and participative versus democratic leaders. In Lewin's experiments, he discovered that the most effective style was democratic. Excessive autocratic styles led to revolution, while under a laissez-faire approach, people were not coherent in their work and did not put in the necessary energy that they did when they were being actively led. Leadership is a knowledge-based game; a game that you win when you have the most knowledge of the subject of leadership. However, the game is just a game until you are in the real world facing real issues with real people. Then the stakes increase and your leadership execution matters. Thus, the perfect leader has a combination of three styles when executing leadership prowess in organizations – Authoritarian, Delegative, and

Participative. Although there is a lot more to leadership effectiveness, focus on these three qualities in your leadership style and watch your success become imminent. Unseasoned or insecure leaders tend toward an Authoritative/Autocratic style in an attempt to demonstrate control. If you find yourself with this tendency, step back and empower your group by loosening control and letting them run with the company mission and vision. Take care of your people and they will take care of your company's mission.

Daniel Goleman, Richard Boyatzis, and Annie McKee identified six emotional leadership styles in their 2002 book "Primal Leadership." Each style has a different effect on people's emotions, and each has strengths and weaknesses in different situations----Visionary, Coaching, Affiliative, Democratic, Pacesetting, and Commanding:

Visionary – new direction

Coaching – developing followers

Affiliative –teamwork emphasis

Democratic – draw upon people's knowledge/skills

Pacesetting – setting high standards for performance

Commanding – crisis management

Four of these styles (Visionary, Coaching, Affiliative, and Democratic) promote harmony and positive outcomes. However, the other two (Commanding and Pacesetting) may create tension and you should only use them in specific circumstances. Leading people incorporates the particular situation involved. When promoting harmony, a leader is presenting a positive environment in which people can strive, and when things are unstable and the environment permits more control, reverting back to commanding and pacesetting may be necessary to get followers back on track. Attempt to keep a positive self-talk by focusing on your strengths to inspire yourself and others. When beginning a project or onboarding a new hire, pacesetting and commanding may be the norm but quickly move away toward the coaching as soon as the follower becomes acclimated to the organization.

After some detailed university studies that detailed a wide array of research, Blake and Mouton, around 1991, surfaced with a Leadership Grid that offered solutions to what they called a Leadership Dilemma. The Managerial Grid by Robert R. Blake and Jane S. Mouton presented a grid that showed both proper and improper leadership styles. Team leadership rose to the top with committed people who felt that they had a "common stake" in the organization. Leaders were found to earn trust and respect at this place in the grid whereas in the other four quadrants, leadership effectiveness was not optimal.

Path-Goal leadership emerged, and this was the first leadership model with theoretical underpinnings that not only directly related to leadership effectiveness but also was tied to empirical research in the area of motivation under the auspices of Expectancy Theory. Based on the situation, the leader was able to select the right behavior to positively affect the follower. Outcomes between leaders and followers seemed to work well according to Path-Goal Theory with increased effort, improved satisfaction, and performance.

Paul Hersey (26 January 1931 - December 18, 2012) was a behavioral scientist and entrepreneur. He was founder of Situational Leadership. Hersey published *Management of Organization Behavior*, which has been developed into several editions. He developed a model similar to Blake and Mouton, but he built in a prescriptive method to applying leadership behavior to both the task and the follower-readiness level. Paul used the last quadrant for delegating in which he turned over responsibility for decisions and implementation. The other styles were for developmental levels similar to Blake and Mouton's Leadership Grid. Both scholars viewed leaders as concern for task and concern for relationship, with delegating holding less concern for task and/or relationship. Paul, however, incorporated the readiness level of the followers and the task in which the follower was selected to engage. Therefore, Situational Leadership offers three tenets that leaders must embrace to be successful. One, determine the task for either the individual or group, second, assess the readiness level of the follower, and finally, pick the most appropriate style at that particular time. The first being tell, then sell, then participate, and the last, as referred to above, delegate.

The sources of management power, which are keys to successful leadership, help leaders select the appropriate style and establish rapport with followers. In a notable study of power conducted by social psychologists John R. P. French and Bertram Raven in 1959, power is divided into five separate and distinct forms. Legitimate Power, which comes from the leader's position in the firm, Reward Power allowing leaders to give or withhold tangible and intangible rewards, Coercive Power providing leaders the ability to punish followers, Expert Power which is based upon special knowledge, skills, and expertise that the leader possesses, and Referent Power which comes from subordinates' and coworkers' respect for the personal characteristics of a leader which earns their loyalty and admiration. Coercive power is used more at the telling stage leadership style while expert uses it at the delegating stage. The consequences of using power are resulting in gaining commitment and compliance or offsetting resistance. Another way to consider this is to look at the spectrum of position power (coercive) to personal power (expert). Leaders have the most success using personal power when developing and leading followers. Even astrological signs have encompassed the art of leadership. If you were born under **CAPRICORN, AQUARIUS, ARIES, or PISCES** you are a natural born leader. Does that mean other signs result in the lack of leadership? Definitely not.

Transformational leadership focuses more on an inspiring style: a partnership has developed, and people are transformed into self-reliant, emotionally mature workers who can accomplish more than they ever thought possible. The state-of-the-art paradigm within leadership is the theory of transformational – transactional leadership proposed by Burns in 1978, who titled the book "Leadership", published by Harper and Row. Following this idea, Bass and Avolio in 2000 published the *MLQ: Multifactor leadership questionnaire* with *Mind Garden*, Incorporated publishers. Over the last two decades, the MLQ has been developed and validated as a true leadership instrument to measure leadership style.

The Bass Transformational Leadership Theory posits that the leader transforms the followers to accomplish more than they would without them. The leader is a role model; Bass used four tenets to explain:

Individual consideration, where the leader coaches, the followers be motivated to complete tasks and improve performance---be a role model.

Intellectual stimulation, provided by a leader to challenge followers and encourage them to learn and grow and disseminate information to the team---inspire and motivate with a vision.

Inspiration by a leader provides an impetus for continuous improvement and higher performance. The leader uses a charismatic approach to inspire greatness; giving the follower the drive to continue progress when the leader is not there, and the follower is working alone or on the team---inspire followers to un-tap their potential.

Idealized influence refers to the leader showing that engaging in continuous development is the right thing to do and will help not only the follower, but the team and all the stakeholders involved---demonstrate genuine concerns for others to bring out their best.

Bernard Bass in his book titled *"Transformational Leadership,"* with Ronald Riggio, published in 2005, shows how Transformational Leadership's focus on the followers helps them realize their leadership potential. Leaders become social architects that affect the culture of the organization---challenges employees to be innovative and creative in their thinking.

"Give a man a fish and you feed him for a day; teach a man to fish and you feed him for a lifetime." -Stephen Covey

When leaders build the transformational leadership relationship with followers, the bonding builds as trust, confidence, and desire continues to grow.

In summary, can you accept the challenge of leadership? Core leadership principles are introduced in this chapter. It is now time to reflect on what you learned and see where you stand in your own personal leadership style. Six-factor leadership is a toolbox filled with ideas and concepts. Even the best tools unopened and unused are useless. Go out and change the world.

CONCLUSION

Leadership is not about you; it is about your people, your followers, your constituents, and your customers. This chapter focused on core leadership principles. The heart of leadership is based on leadership theory and practice, but the real leadership is in the workplace, in the field, on the hospital floor, and on the front lines of any customer service job.

Mastering the concepts of leadership are as easy as any other skill but it takes practice. Remember to use all six pillars when practicing leadership but focus heavily on the models that are introduced in this chapter.

KEY TAKEAWAYS

1. As a colleague of mine once said, David Wolf, Interim Dean of The School of Professional and Career Education, "Run it like you own it!" The benefits of working for someone else gives you the opportunity to run-it-like-you-own-it and still go home at night without worrying about losing it. The only key to success is productivity and performance. Leaders are social architects that use all their skills to build a great cultural environment. As Peter Drucker once said, "Culture eats strategy for breakfast." True, but strategy will help a leader develop the right culture with sustainable value for all stakeholders.

2. Situational Leadership is one of the paramount models of leadership. Transformational Leadership has also received a great deal of traction over the past few decades. Authentic Leadership has a true spirit of individuality to it also. Path Goal Theory is the only theoretical model that stands the test of time in the academic circles today. Your goal is to pick a leadership model or theory and use it to the best of your ability. Remember the people that you need also need you, and in order to lead them, you need a strong leadership presence.

3. Search through movies and novels and look for leadership characteristics. Learn about the leaders that are great and those that may have thought they were great but led the "Black Hat" of leadership style. Black Hat leaders are very charismatic and have a cause, that they very well

may be true but is wrong in many ways. Learn what to do as a leader and also what not to do.

4. Develop a strong sense of discernment. Remember that with your experience and knowledge you are unique and a real asset to your career, your profession, your personal life, and your followers. Discernment is knowing ahead of time what to think, what to feel, and most importantly, what to do. With discernment, you can manifest the ability to make smart judgments and decisions. When selecting followers to be leaders and developing them, you can use discernment to pick the best candidate and use onboarding to develop them. One City Manager of Boynton Beach once mentioned that he sends a letter indicating that a follower was selected for leadership, sends them to graduate school for leadership training using the Situational Leadership model, and prepares them for leadership. Thus, discernment describes a wise way of judging between things, or a particularly perceptive way of seeing things. While the dictionary vocabulary dot com has stated an excellent definition, Nonaka and Takeuchi, two seasoned leaders, captured the true essence of discernment in their article, "The Big Idea: The Wise Leader" in May 2011. Become a phronetic leader.

"Never did we expect more of leadership—and never have we been so wrong.... Phronetic leaders practice moral discernment about what's good and act on it in every day." -Ikujiro Nonaka and Hirotaka Takeuchi

6

Pillar 6: Leadership and Change

"If you don't know where you're going, any road will take you there. A clear destination is necessary to guide the journey of change. Many change efforts falter because of confusion over exactly where everyone is expected to arrive. In the children's book, Alice in Wonderland, Alice, who is confused anyway, asks the Cheshire cat which road she should take. The magical cat responds with this helpful reminder to pin down your goal first. Zoom in on the destination on your mental map, and then zoom out to pick the best path." ____Rosabeth Moss Kantor

The question most people ask today is, "Why do people resist change?" Most people respond to this question with a feeling of uncomfortableness. One reason is that resisting change projects a sense of insecurity, and in some cases, a low self-esteem. We all know that the only thing constant is change.

The biggest problem with the resistance to change begins at the top and trickles down in the form of inertia.

If we keep on doing what we have always done before, we will always get what we always got before NOW!

Inertia builds momentum, which trickles down to the timing of the change that places people in panic mode along with surprise, peer-pressure, and a complete misunderstanding and lack of communication of why the change is important. In addition, people feel a loss of control that makes them unsettled when it comes to change efforts.

Jim Carrey in "Liar Liar" places his biggest desire to lie as a professional attribute that causes him to resist change in one of his famous scenes about when the pen is blue, but he would like to say that it is 'red.'

The biggest problem with the resistance to change begins at the top and trickles down in the form of inertia.

Kotter, in his article titled *"Leading Change: Why Transformation Efforts Fail,"* in the *Harvard Business Review* found that there are eight steps to leading change:

- Establish a sense of urgency

- Form powerful guiding coalition

- Create a vision

- Communicate the vision

- Empower others to act on the vision

- Plan for and create short-term wins

- Consolidate improvements and produce more change

- Institutionalize change(ing)

Susan Campbell, author of the book titled "From Chaos to Confidence," published by Simon and Shuster (1995) argues that people have a tendency to feel unsettled because they perceive that something is not right. They then go through a stage of denial, indicating that it may not be so bad. Finally, one day, they face the present moment and see things the way they are as opposed to the way they wish them to be.

Then, an 'Aha' moment arises in which we begin to let go because we realize that the past is not working even though the future is unclear. This is where Susan offers the best advice by encouraging us to envision what we want, knowing that we want something. Then, we begin to explore new options thinking that maybe we can do it if we give it a try. Similar to the Expectancy Theory of Motivation, perception is reality. Finally, we commit to some type of action and realize that deep down inside we can do what it is we have in mind. Best of all, Susan tells us to integrate the change by doing it. So go out and "Just do it" as the "Nike" logo entails.

John Kotter is a highly recognized scholar on the subject of leadership. He talks about how to win over both hearts and minds in his book titled "The Heart of Change: Real-Life Stories of How People Change Their Organizations" published in 2012. Kotter and Cohen mention an Eight Step Process about how to always win hearts and minds. Their ideas are an important part of business thinking and a way to change behavior in an organizational or a cultural change.

They argue that emotions of business must play an important role to change behavior to achieve the significant change projects. Getting to the business heart is something that many people miss.

Kotter is worth noting for executives. Here are four steps to lead charismatically:

Step 1: Articulate an appealing vision that can inspire action.

Step 2: Link the present with a better future through the vision.

Step 3: Communicate high performance expectations and express the necessary confidence that followers can perceive that they can attain them.

Step 4: Enhance follower self-esteem, self-efficacy, and self-confidence---always moving the focus of leadership away from you, the leader, to the follower.

Step 5: Convey a new set of values and set an example for followers to imitate or relate to. Always be continuously improving.

Step 6: Make self-sacrifices and engage in unconventional behavior to demonstrate courage and convictions about the vision. Think outside the box and take risks within reason.

    I was fortunate to meet a great leader as he made a presentation at an Academy of Management conference. His view of leadership is profound. Kevin Roberts, the CEO of the Worldwide Saatchi & Saatchi created an ideas company. Kevin instills Emotional Intelligence in his followers and argues that nothing is impossible. Kevin Roberts is CEO Worldwide of ideas company Saatchi & Saatchi, one of the world's largest and most successful creative organizations, handling more than fifty of the world's most valuable global brands. Heading a team of more than seven thousand people in eighty-two countries, Roberts led Saatchi & Saatchi to become both Advertising Age and Adweek magazines' Global Agency Network of the Year in 2003. He is the author of the best-selling book "*Lovemarks: the future beyond brands,*" (powerHouse Books, 2004), which has now been translated into fourteen languages, with more than 150,000 copies in print. He states:

Consider turning around your organization by focusing on the topline not the bottom, on inspiration not leadership, on performance, not promises, on employees, not stakeholders, on turning existing constituents into guests, on the work not the process, on teamwork not on individuals. *-Kevin Roberts*

Kevin pointed out an idea that is brilliant. He quotes a neurologist named Donald Calne in his book, "Within Reason: Rationality and Human Behavior," written in 2010. Kevin states Calne's quote brilliantly:

"The essential difference between emotion and reason is that emotion leads to action while reason leads to conclusions." -Donald Calne

The point here is to grab the attention of people through emotion, and once you have done that, then you have reached both their heart and mind. Think of walking into a car dealership – a car dealership of your choice – chances are after seeing the car that you love; you may buy it on impulse. Why? Because the emotional connection supersedes the wallet and justifies your need to feel that you have accomplished something worthwhile to you and that you have what is sometimes called "Arrived." You see, our car is an extension of our ego and in some cases, buying the car may be a sense of accomplishment. Ergo, emotion leads to buying the car on the spot because sleeping on the idea would forfeit a car sale as one reason with the idea itself lingering too long.

Calne connects this idea with what Kevin calls "Lovemarks." Whom better than Tom Peters, the management guru himself can promote Kevin's book?

"Ideas move mountains, especially in turbulent times. Lovemarks is the product of the fertile-iconoclast mind of Kevin Roberts, CEO Worldwide of Saatchi & Saatchi. Roberts argues vociferously, and with a ton of data to support him, that traditional branding practices have become stultified. What's needed are customer Love affairs. Roberts lays out his grand scheme for mystery, magic, sensuality, and the like in his gloriously designed book Lovemarks." –Tom Peters

Read this book if you want to learn more about Kevin's Lovemarks idea.

The key point is that Kevin swapped command and control for unleash and inspire. Here are Kevin's own words from a conference at the Academy of Management, a group of management scholars that gather yearly from around the globe. Being a Manager or even a Leader is just another label. Stepping up to being an INSPIRER of Emotional Intelligence – demands personal transformation as a part of organizational transformation.

Inspiration unlocks human potential
Inspiration is non-coercive
Inspiration is non-hierarchical
Inspiration is viral and contagious
Inspiration builds to a tipping point
Beyond inspiration, there is magic
Inspiration takes you from mediocre performance through high Performance to Peak Performance.

LEADERSHIP CHANGE

When it comes to change, one scholar to consider is Jack Gabarro. In his book, "The Dynamics of Taking Charge," published by Harvard Business Review in May-June 1985, came up with a change mantra.

- **Taking Hold**: Too many people are busy picking the low hanging fruit.

- **Immersion**: Learning what else to do instead is the way-to-go.
- **Reshaping**: Major change efforts may be in order.
- **Consolidation**: Once you make the change, settling in.
- **Refinement:** Remember, even the Tin Man needed oil - fine-tuning.

Never forget the brilliance of Emotional Intelligence, covered earlier in the book. Continue to recognize your own emotions and tune in to not only your own but other people's emotions too---especially followers. Now that you have a handle on your emotions, try managing them. Develop a strong self-talk to get out of Emotional Hijackings and keep yourself focused. Always, and I mean always, pay attention to your "Self-Awareness." For more on this topic, read *Emotional Intelligence* by Daniel Goleman, published in 1995.

Many leaders remember Doug McGregor. One of my colleagues actually had him as a professor in college and he was embraced my leaders worldwide, One kernel that I would like to present here is knowing that, as a leader, you are always teaching. For more on this topic, read Douglas MacGregor, *The Human Side of Enterprise*. Here is a quote from pages 199-200:

Every encounter between a superior and a subordinate involves learning of some kind for the subordinate. (It should involve learning for the superior, too, but that is another matter.) When the boss gives an order, asks for a job to be done, reprimands, praises, conducts an appraisal interview, deals with a mistake, holds a staff meeting, works with his subordinates in solving a problem, gives a salary increase, discusses a possible promotion, or takes any other action with subordinates, he is teaching them something. The attitudes, the habits, the expectations of the subordinate will be either reinforced or modified to some degree as a result of every encounter with the boss . . . The day-by-day experience of the job is so much more powerful that it tends to overshadow what the individual may learn in other settings.

Michael Eisner in a 1994 annual report stated, "We cannot stop it and we cannot escape it. We can let it destroy us or we can embrace it. We must embrace it." We can do this by making learning a continuous process that is fruitful for both the leader and follower. Kurt Lewin embraced change with his simple model. Kurt's book titled "Resolving Social Conflicts: Field Theory in Social Science," published on Feb 1, 1997, gave way to a simple but effective model:

- Unfreeze – make some sought of radical change
- Retrain – minimize the resistance to change by limiting disruption
- Refreeze – attempt to make the change permanent

My friend and colleague, Jim Clawson, at the University of Virginia, argues that we may need to retool often in the form of retraining, even after we refreeze---especially as new people are new or onboarding. Change involves getting people to embrace leadership progress as it unfolds; they need to feel empowered by the change-effort and remain engaged in the decision-making process to help put the change-effort into practice.

In many cases, inertia sets in, and people get off track.

Working inside a box limits potential and causes corporate hyperventilation and stagnation. Unfreezing melts down the potential negative actions and causation of aberration in performance levels. People begin to drop bad habits and cumbersome ways of completing tasks and open up a whole new perspective to change. Now the change process can begin. After the organizational change is in play, there may be some sort of resistance by some people. As mentioned earlier in the chapter, change is embraced at times with some form of resistance. Leaders can overcome this by communication and education. The fact of the matter is, with any effort, change, or the perception of it, will only reach its full potential if it's embraced and made somewhat permanent. Somewhat because change is always a constantly moving target, thus "re-freezing" provides the new structure of the change to manifest. Lewin mentioned "freeze" as the opposite of unfreeze. In 1947, Lewin wrote that change efforts in and of themselves may not be enough. He indicates that it does not suffice to define the objective of planned change in group performance as the reaching of a different level. Permanency of the new level, or permanency for a desired period, should be included in the objective.

For more on this idea, read his work titled "Frontiers in Group Dynamics" published in 1947. There are many critics, especially given the years of initiation being almost seventy-five. In spite of this minor flaw, Kurt Lewin's change theory is still valid today.

A great scholar by the name of Kotter From (excerpted from Leading Change, John Kotter, HBS Press, 1996) drove the 8-point leadership model home when he found both the 8 errors of ineffective leadership and then turned them inside out for the 8 effective leadership stages. Here are the ineffective ones.

- Allowing complacency
- Failing to create a guiding coalition
- Underestimating the power of vision
- Under-communicating the vision
- Allowing Obstacles to block the vision
- Failing to create short-term wins
- Declaring victory too soon
- Neglecting to anchor changes in culture

As executives, think and ponder on these eight ineffective leadership modes of operation and zigzag through them to avoid mediocrity. According to Kotter, in order to create the transformation using the eight-step process, remember that transformation is a process and not an event.

Peter Senge, in his book titled "The Necessary Revolution: How Individuals and Organizations Are Working Together to Create a Sustainable World," published in 2010, he explains why companies succeed and indicate why some fail. He authored this book with Bryan Smith, Nina Kruschwitz, Joe Laur, and Sara Schley. These authors argue that major change agents need to focus on the future and determine what they need to do for tomorrow and who they need to partner with. Leaders that only focus on what they are doing today fail to reap the opportunities available to them and their organization.

Jim Clawson expressed his approach to leadership in a simple and impactful way in his book titled "Level Three Leadership: Getting below the Surface," published by Prentice Hall (January 17, 2011). He summarizes leadership in an easy to follow and easy to master way:

Help people get out of their comfort zones (habits)

Be willing to deliver disconfirming data

Identify and collaborate with like-minded groups

Be willing to help people through pain and denial

Help people identify alternative approaches (creativity, innovation)

Help people plan their experiments (active coaching)

Help interpret results data from experiments (encouragement)

Reward and reinforce successes (encouragement)

Be relentless in reinforcement

Behave consistently all the time

Summary

The key is to encourage the "Enterprise Mindset" which provides a sense that "we're all in this together"---- supports organization-wide accountability and provides a consistent corporate message. An entrepreneurial drive keeps employees focused on and motivated by the corporate vision. Leaders who model positive, successful behaviors and make it safe for employees to explore their ideas---encouraging the what-if ideas to flourish, inspire people.

As Robert Fritz's states in his book, "The Path of Least Resistance: Learning to Become the Creative Force in Your Own Life," published by Butterworth-Heinemann (May15, 1998):

> *1. Describe accurately where you are.*
> *(Collins: Good to Great: Why Some Companies Make the Leap...And Others Don't…..SAYS…."confront the brutal facts")*
> *2. Make a vision of what you want to create with your life/work. Make sure it is something you want so bad; you are magnetically attracted to it.*
> *3. Formally choose the result you want.*
> *4. Move on (if you really want it, you will naturally 'flow' in that direction.)*

After following these four steps, as Clawson states, "What do you want to create?" Make sure that you take care of yourself as a leader so that you can run on all eight cylinders.

Re-energize with retreats and fun activities.
Reward yourself and those around you both verbally and with small tokens of appreciation.
Develop positive relationships.
Rejuvenate, challenge, and invigorate your staff and yourself with creativity.
Give and receive recognition.
Revisit your roots – go back to the mission.
Reassess your goals and plan—be flexible.

Examine personal growth and continuing education.
Take time out for vacation and encourage staff to do so as well.
Make it a lifestyle decision. Choose to enjoy what you do and set healthy and necessary boundaries to keep it enjoyable and fulfilling.

*** The End ****

KEY TAKEAWAYS

1. The squeaky wheel gets the grease! Unfortunately, it is true that the kid that cries loudest is fed first. However, the kid does not get respect. You as a leader are an agent of change and you want to assert yourself and communicate well but think of emotional intelligence and when to be quiet and just listen to others.
2. Mobilize, leverage, and expand your network. Ben Franklin was able to focus on continuous improvement.

Benjamin Franklin's 13 Virtues

Franklin tracked his progress on charts he created. The first letter of each day was listed on the top and the first letter of each virtue was indicated down the left side. He would add a dot if he felt he fell short of meeting that virtue on a given day. Benjamin Franklin carried these charts with him as a reminder of his personal plan of conduct. Franklin provides the following 13 virtues, which continue to be relevant today. Next to each virtue is Franklin's definition. Underneath is a leadership and change idea to contemplate.

1. Temperance ("Eat not to dullness and drink not to elevation.")
Express your opinion and leadership presence when necessary but remember to be emotional intelligent and use self-awareness by being an authentic leader.

2. Silence ("Speak not but what may benefit others or yourself. Avoid trifling conversation.") Avoid water-cooler talk, especially in contentious situations. Do not speak critically of others.

3. Order ("Let all your things have their places. Let each part of your business have its time.") Create order in everything you do. Structure and strategy are key attributes of leadership.

4. Resolution ("Resolve to perform what you ought. Perform without fail what you resolve.") Always be on time. Give yourself enough time to develop, plan, and take into consideration obstacles before

they appear. Fear of change can sidetrack you but also ensure you know your shortfall and plan for it.

5. Frugality ("Make no expense but to do good to others or yourself: i.e., Waste nothing.") Recycle your ideas. Everything you do can be written about and formulated into an article or case study that someone can learn from.

6. Industry ("Lose no time. Be always employed in something useful. Cut off all unnecessary actions.") Create several jobs for yourself. Hobbies, extracurricular activities such as writing or performing as an actor or artist. Develop your craft to be the best it can be. Never slack off and let a day go by without taking something from it that is positive and will help you grow. Use your time more productively.

7. Sincerity ("Use no hurtful deceit. Think innocently and justly; and, if you speak, speak accordingly.") Make the conscious choice every day to be sincere, honest, and show high integrity.

8. Justice ("Wrong none, by doing injuries or omitting the benefits that are your duty.") Remember to always be in the right place at the right time and not vice versa. Be careful whom you run with. Be

diligent in keeping your character and never sign any political document without realizing the consequences later. Remember, everything you do is public today.

9. Moderation ("Avoid extremes. Forebear resenting injuries so much as you think they deserve.") Remember that everything in moderation is better than being self-indulgent.

10. Cleanliness ("Tolerate no uncleanness in body, clothes or habitation.") There are only so many things we can do as leaders to be the best we can be. Do them all and do not slack off. Keep your office, car, and home clean and organized.

11. Chastity ("Rarely use venery but for health or offspring; Never to dullness, weakness, or the injury of your own or another's peace or reputation.") Remember to honor the people in your life. As Elton sings, "I am thankful for the people that came into my life." Respect them whether they are with you or not.

12. Tranquility ("Be not disturbed at trifles, or at accidents common or unavoidable.") Balance both work and play and do both at your highest performance. Remember your loved ones and

praise your boss and company that provides you with sustenance and livelihood.

13. Humility ("Imitate Jesus and Socrates.") Stand on the shoulders of the giants.

Are you ready to accept the 13-Week Self Improvement Challenge?

Final Thoughts...

- There are two kinds of people in this world...those who lead and those who follow. Which one are you and with whom do you surround yourself?

- When someone comes to you with a problem, you have a glass half full or a glass half empty—one with negative energy about to be drained and the other one full of life and sustenance. Do you look solely at the problem and make matters worse or resolve the problem and create optimal solution?

- When faced with an urgent situation, be the most silent person in the room and act non-emotionally. People often want to react with the same modality in which crisis hits—do not model behavior;

change it. Slow the unwelcomed nervousness down and make optimal decisions that will benefit the entire group.

According to an article by Berman titled "The Three Essential Warren Buffett quotes to live by," written by Forbes Magazine in 2014, my three favorite Buffett quotes to live by:

1. "It takes 20 years to build a reputation and five minutes to ruin it. If you think about that, you'll do things differently."

2. "Risk comes from not knowing what you're doing."

3. "You only have to do a very few things right in your life so long as you don't do too many things wrong."

What leadership contribution can I make without quoting Warren Buffett? Remember, do not walk on eggshells but always be sober and know your surroundings. It is better to be in an uncomfortable situation at times to learn and grow than be in a position that is known and stagnant. Use the ten-finger rule --- attempt to do nine things right before you do one thing slightly wrong.

When running-up against difficult people, remember that you too may have been difficult at one point or other in your life, so be empathetic and help them get back on track like perhaps someone did for you when you needed it. A management scholar by the name of Quinn in his book "Deep Change" tells a story about the dead tadpole; the frogs that can leap jumped out of the boiling water and left the others to swim for survival. The others eventually turned to tadpoles that boiled to death. Consider the boiled frog story as lesson learned and how it may manifest in your own life. Have you been swimming in the wrong pond? If so, remember that the fastest swimmers jump ship first so take a leap and get on with your leadership.

TEN LEADERSHIP THINGS TO DO RIGHT NOW!

- When faced with intense professional scrutiny, remember it is not who wins the fight that wins the war. People like winners but hate losing wars. Try not to go to war at all.

- Accelerate your wins and limit your mistakes. However, mistakes may happen, so keep trying---never give up!

- Hire and lead motivated people. Find them while they are motivated and build upon their motivation. If you cannot find them motivated, then engage them to attempt to motivate them in every way possible.

  - Every time you take advantage of one person, you lose the regard for another person. Remember that people are always looking around them, always comparing themselves to others, and always perceptive to your actions. Act accordingly.

- Great mentors are able to find mentees. Find followers and help them at that level or move them up the Maslow Hierarchy; never oppress them or hold them back.

- It is not what you do in life; it is what you leave behind. Make sure you are always building a great legacy. Develop your legacy while you are alive.

- Give back to people less fortunate than you—Pay-It-Backwards whenever possible. The people you influence will remember to do the same.

- Never stop growing. Your mind is a powerful resource that needs nurturing, but you must have fun doing this or it becomes a chore—reinvent yourself if you have to but use staying power to commit to your career.

- Leaders open doors by showing rather than doing. The more you facilitate, the better your followers will learn. Walk the talk and remember MBWA – Management By Walking Around.

- When you wake up in the morning, be happy. It is your choice every day! Help others to do the same too. Remember to help the least among us at all times and that will make you feel better about yourself as a person in society and as a leader in your profession and personal life.

The End

This Book is the Beginning of
Your New Leadership –
LEVEL-UP LEADERSHIP!

***

Selected Bibliography for Future Reading

Alderfer, C. P. *Existence, relatedness, and growth.* New York: Free Press, 1972.

Herzberg, F. *Work and the nature of man.* Cleveland: World Publishing, 1966.

Herzberg, F., Mausner, B., & Snyderman, B. B. *The motivation to work.* New York: Wiley, 1959.

Maslow, A. H. *Motivation and personality.* New York: Harper & Row, 1954.

Maslow, A. H. *Toward a Theory of Being.* New York: Van Nostrand Reinhold, 1968.

McClelland, D. C. *The achieving society.* Princeton, N. J.: Van Nostrand, 1961.

McClelland, D. C. Business drive and national achievement. *Harvard Business Review*, 1962.

McClelland, D. C. Achievement motivation can be developed. *Harvard Business Review*, 1965a, 43, 6-24, 178.

McClelland, D. C. Toward a theory of motive acquisition. *American Psychologist, 1965b, 20, 321-333.*

McClelland, D. C. *Assessing Human Motivation.* New York: Appelton-Century-Crofts, 1953.

Porter L. W., & Lawler, E. E. III. *Managerial attitudes and performance.* Richard D. Irwin, 1968.

Vroom, V. H. *Work and motivation.* New York: Wiley, 1964.

Locke, E. A (1996). Motivating through conscious goal setting, Applied and Preventive Psychology, 5, 117-124.

Lewin, K., Dembo, T., Festinger, L., & Sears, P.S. (1944). Level of inspiration: In J. McV.
Hunt (Ed.). Personality and Behavioral Disorders (vol. 1, Pp. 333-378, New York: Ronald.

Bargh, J.A., & Chartrand, T. L. (1999). The unbearable auto-maticity of being. American Psychologist, 54:7, 462-479.

Wegner, D. M., & Wheatley, T. (1999). Apparent mental causation: Sources of the experience of will. American Psychologist, 54/7, 480-492.

Harackiewicz, J.M., Samsone, C., and Maderlink , G (1985). Competence, achievement orientation, and intrinsic motivation: A process analysis. Journal of Personality and Social Psychology, 48, 493-508.

Baddaracco, J. L. (2006). "Leadership in literature: A conversation with business ethicist Joseph L. Badaracco, Jr." Harvard Business Review.

Bass, B. M. (1985). Leadership and performance beyond expectation. New York: New York Press Publishers.

Bass, B. M. (1990). "From transactional to transformational leadership: Learning to share the vision,"

Organizational Dynamics: 19-31.

Bass, B. M., Avolio, B. J., and Goodheim, L. (1987). "Biography and assessment of transformational leadership at the world class level," Journal of Management, 13, 7-19.

Bash, L. (2003). Adult learners in the academy. Anker Publishing Company, Inc.
Coleman, D. (1998). What makes a leader? Harvard Business Review, 76 (6): 93-102.

Conger and Kanungo, (1987). "Toward a behavioral theory of charismatic leadership in organizational settings, "Academy of Management Review, 12 (4):637-647.

Crom, J. O. (1990, January). What's new in leadership? Executive Excellence, 7, 15-16.

Duluga, (1988). "Relationship of transformational and transactional leadership with employee

influencing strategies," Group and Organizational Studies, 13 (4):456-467.
Dreamworks Pictures (2001). The Last Castle, Dreamworks Home Entertainment, 100 Universal City Plaza, Universal City, CA 91608.

Gibb, C. A. (1954). Leadership. In Gardner L. (Ed.), handbook of social psychology, Reading, MA: Addison-Wesley.

Hersey, P. and Blanchard, K. (1996). Management of organizational behavior: Utilizing human resources, 7th ed. Englewood Cliffs, NJ: Prentice Hall.

Hersey, P. and Blanchard, K. (1996). Great ideas revisited:

Revisiting the life-cycle theory of leadership. Training and Development, 50 (1):42-47.

House (1996). Path-goal theory of leadership: Lessons, legacy, and a reformulated theory," The Leadership Quarterly, 7 (3): 323-352.

Jenning, E. E. (1961). The anatomy of leadership. Management of Personnel Quarterly, 1 (1): 2-10.

Kirkpatrick, S. A. and Locke, E. A. (1991). Leadership: Do traits matter? Academy of Management Executive 5 (2):44-57.

Knowles, M. S. (1980). The modern practice of adult education: From pedagogy to andragogy. New York, NY: Cambridge Books.

Knowles, M. S. (1984). Andragogy in action: Applying modern principles of adult learners. San Francisco, CA: Jossey-Bass.

MacKeracher, D. (2004). Making sense of adult learning. Toronto: University of Toronto Press.

Pawar, B. S., and Eastman, K. K. (1997). The nature and implications of contextual influences on transformational leadership: A conceptual examination. Academy of Management Review, 22: 80-99.

Podsadoff, MacKenzie, Moorman, and Fetter, (1990). "Transformational leader behaviors and their effects on followers' trust in leader, satisfaction, and organizational citizenship behaviors," The Leadership Quarterly, 1 (2):107-42.

Provitera, M. J. "The Last Castle Video Case Study: Applying Leadership Theory," Management Case Study Journal, Vol. 7, No. 1, 2007: 78-82.

Stogdill, R. M. (1948, January). Personal factors associated with leadership: A survey of the literature. Journal of Psychology, 25: 35-64.

Stogdill, R. M. (1974). Handbook of leadership. New York: Free Press.
Tracy, J. B., and Hinkin, T. R. (1998, September). Transformational leadership or effective managerial practices? Groups and Organizational Management, 23 (3): 220. Thousand Oaks, CA: Sage.

COMPLIMENTARY CASE STUDIES

The Wizard of Oz and Dorothy's Level-UP Leadership

Dr. Michael J. Provitera, Management Consultant,
Business Book Author, Management Professor

Published 9-11-2018 (All Rights Reserved)

Copyright ®Dr. Michael J. Provitera September 11, 2018

In the film *The Wizard of Oz,* Dorothy learned how to be a leader by means of experience coupled with sheer necessity. It was because of her need to avoid her fears and apprehension that led her to leadership excellence. Leaders can learn a lot from *The Wizard of Oz.* In the midst of a life struggle, Dorothy, the protagonist, found herself living a mediocre life, one that she was unsure of with limited opportunity to grow and learn. When a tornado swept through Kansas, her homeland, her house was swept up and dropped in the middle of the Wicked Witch of the East, the antagonist. Her competitors grew as the Wicked Witch's sister is now out for vengeance. Her need for change opened up a more competitive environment for her; one that she had to face head on, or she could never return home to her safe, warm, and loving family. She has to plan her way back home. Recognizing a need for change, Glinda, the Good Witch of the West, comes to her rescue with ruby slippers; unfortunately, this is not enough. Glinda sends Dorothy on her way to meet the Wizard of Oz with her dog Toto. Taking action, her quest to see the Wizard begins with the first step on the Yellow Brick Road. She is in a strange place with nothing but her mission and vision. At last, she finds hope in a team of followers: a Scarecrow, a Tin Man, and a Lion. With teamwork, they find solace in each other's attributes and compensate for each other's faults. A field of poppies awaits them and places them into a slumber. The flying monkeys attack and a haunted forest awaits them. By overcoming these obstacles, Dorothy and her followers manifest their way through the heroic Yellow Brick Road. Upon reaching the Oz and the Wizard, the Wizard does not grant her wish to return home and challenges them to ascertain the Wicked Witch's broom. Direction is key in this quest; they must head West, a land of unfamiliar territory and a quest that appears to be nothing less than treacherous. However, they rise to the occasion, pursue forward, and overcome challenges faced upon them. Dorothy and her group almost reach a demise at the witch's castle as she is about to be incarcerated while the hourglass counts the time to her death. Grasping at a struggle to save the scarecrow now on fire, Dorothy tosses a bucket of water to save the scarecrow, not knowing that this will melt the wicked witch. We often face times of warfare in business as companies and rivals attempt to outdo us with technology and advertising. The scarecrow was an easy victim for the witch who knew a little fire would set him aflame. Dorothy is awarded the broomstick and heads back to Oz. The diverse nature of the group led to decisions that would not have existed otherwise. Dorothy did not know that water would melt the witch as she attempted to save her colleague. Upon returning to Oz, a meeting of the minds take place only to find that the Wizard is a fake, a fraud, a gimmick to get the broom and selfishly protect his world from the evil witch. The Wizard attempts to return to Oz in a haphazard hot air balloon and leaves Dorothy and Toto behind by accident.

The Wizard had a self-publicity awareness that led others to believe that he was better than they were and that he could lead them. This was all built upon a perception of being greater and more powerful than others are. Leaders that possess a manipulative way to help others become more successful in what is sometimes called a "High Mach," based upon Nicolo Machiavelli's book *The Prince*. Having an awareness of how to help others help themselves is a trait that a leader can possess, as long as it is used with high integrity, and it is ethical. Authentic leaders know who they are and who they are not. In this case, the Wizard was a fraud. However, leaders can attempt to learn and develop skills that can make them stand out amongst their followers and build credibility. In that sense, he *was* great and powerful. In the midst of the faulty attempt to return Dorothy to Kansas, Glinda appears and reminds her that the ruby slippers are her way home by clicking them together like a magic wand. Dorothy remembered then that the slippers were always available to her and missed that detail because she was caught up in the excitement of challenge, mystery, and enchantment. Dorothy awakens from her dream and experiences a new world, one that she would never want to leave. She gained a new appreciation for what she once had, and thought was lost forever. She realized she had much more than anyone can imagine right at home; as her famous line was, "There is no place like home."

Case Study Questions for Discussion

Questions 1 - Professional Communication and Authentic Leadership

a. How did Dorothy prepare herself for leadership?
b. How did Dorothy start leading by taking on new challenges?

c. How did Dorothy start seeking opportunities to spread her leadership wisdom to the Tin Man, Lion, Scarecrow, and even the Wizard himself?
d. How did Dorothy's learning process continue even after her return home?

Questions 2 – Decision Making

a. How did Dorothy get the group to come up with the new idea to save her in the castle from the wicked witch?
b. How did Dorothy concentrate resources where they were needed and where were the likely payoffs of these resources the greatest?
c. How did Dorothy single out the key followers as influencers (i.e., the Tin Man, Scarecrow, and the Lion) and did she use that person's strengths to help her reach the Land of Oz, retrieve the broom, and defeat the evil witch?

Question 3 - Motivating People

a. How did the Wizard of Oz apply the motivational force theory?
b. Determine what outcomes are important to Dorothy, the Tin Man, the Scarecrow, and the Lion?
c. How did the Wizard know how to address individual preferences?
d. Did he tie the desired outcome to the reward for Dorothy, the Tin Man, the Scarecrow, and the Lion? Yes, or no?
e. Did the Wizard of Oz ensure that the connection between each of their (Dorothy, Tin Man, Scarecrow, Lion) performance and rewards were communicated well right from the beginning? If yes, explain. If no, why not?

f. How can you personally develop a mindset that includes the "What is in it for me" for yourself?

Question 4 - Managing People – Tap into your emotional intelligence

There are three ancient, yet still-used persuasive appeals. The first persuasive appeal is ***Ethos***, an ethical appeal; used to show an audience that you are a credible source who is worth listening to. If you wanted to research, you can find a credible source (people) to build your example. The second persuasive appeal is ***Pathos***, an emotional appeal; used to get the audience to feel what you want them to feel. This is about choosing the right words and tone to draw pity, inspire followers, and prompt the audience to action. When doing research, pathos uses arguments and debates using emotions to trigger people to be on your side. The third persuasive appeal is ***Logos***, a logical appeal; used to convince the audience that you are logical, and your message is well reasoned. When doing research, you can use numbers and codes that are not too complicated like percents, decimals, and fractions to persuade people. For example, 95% of companies now use Six Sigma in our industry and only 5% are using the Total Quality Management model of the 80s.

a. Did Dorothy use any of the three ancient persuasive skills? If yes, when and how?
b. Did the Wizard use the three ancient persuasive skills? If so, when and how?
c. Develop an appeal for your followers using one of the three persuasive appeals above. Make it at least a one-paragraph answer with the first and last sentence

connecting the paragraph with the middle sentence(s) in the center of the paragraph.

Question 5 Leading People

a. Has Dorothy exemplified the situational leadership style model of leadership? Has she used different styles of leadership for each different follower-leader relationship:
- Telling (Provide specific instructions and closely supervise performance)
- Selling (Explain decisions and provide opportunity for clarification)
- Participating (Share ideas and facilitate in making decisions)
- Delegating (Turn over responsibility for decisions and implementation)
Each situational leadership style above can be explained using a different part of the film. The key is to learn how Dorothy uses her leadership styles appropriately.

b. Which source of power did Dorothy and/or the Wizard use in any of the movie scenes? (Legitimate Power, Reward Power, Coercive Power, Expert Power, Referent Power) Explain.
- Legitimate Power
  The authority that a manager has by virtue of his or her position in the firm.
  Example: the power to hire or fire employees.
- Reward Power
  The ability of a manager to give or withhold tangible and intangible rewards.
  Example: awarding pay raises or providing verbal praise for good performance.

Effective managers use reward power to signal to employees that they are doing a good job.
- Coercive Power
The ability of a manager to punish others.
Examples: verbal reprimand, pay cuts, and dismissal
Limited in effectiveness and application; can have serious negative side effects.
- Expert Power
Power that is based on special knowledge, skills, and expertise that the leader possesses.
First-line and middle managers have the most expert power; most often consists of technical ability.
- Referent Power
Power that comes from subordinates and coworkers' respect for the personal characteristics of a leader, which earns their loyalty and admiration. Usually held by and available for use by likable managers who are concerned about their workers.

Question 6 Leadership and Change

a. John Kotter came up with eight concepts to manage change. Has Dorothy used any of them? If so, which one? When?

Establish a sense of urgency

Create a guiding coalition

Develop strong vision and strategy

Over communicate the vision and strategy

Redesign to encourage broad-based action

Generate short-term wins

Consolidate gains in redesign and HR

Anchor changes in the culture

b. Professor Emeritus James Clawson, University of Virginia, Darden School of Business, developed a way to manage change with a behavioral approach using both knowledge and compassion. Dr. Clawson is the author of the book titled "*Level Three Leadership: Getting Below the Surface*," (5th Edition). Has Dorothy and/or the Wizard used any of these tenets of leading change?

Help people get out of their comfort zones (habits)
Be willing to deliver disconfirming data
Identify and collaborate with like-minded groups
Be willing to help people through pain and denial
Help people identify alternative approaches (creativity, innovation)
Help people plan their experiments (active coaching)
Help interpret results data from experiments (encouragement)
Reward and reinforce successes (encouragement)
Be relentless in reinforcement
Behave consistently all the time

***FEATURED CASE STUDY** – Jackson Breaks: Level-Up Leadership*

Jackson Breaks: Level-Up Leadership

Dr. Michael J. Provitera, Management Consultant, Business Book Author, Management Professor

Published 9-11-2018 (All Rights Reserved)

Copyright ®Dr. Michael J. Provitera September 11, 2018

Copy only with permission by the author (email; website)

docprov@msn.com

http://docprov.com

Jackson, known as Jack, ran out of his home office with a staggering leap. He was on his work-from-home day which is one out of five; a new approach on the Financial Sector to cut costs in the high-rising buildings of Manhattan, New York, USA. He does not have a nanny and his daughter was home from public school due to a Jewish holiday. He got a call from his commercial bank human resource manager Shelly Goldman. "How do you feel about taking on a leadership role in Wisconsin?" she asked quite abruptly----almost expecting an answer on the spot. Jack felt a chill in the bottom of his stomach that ached. "Umm..." he said, "can I have twenty-four hours to think about it?"

Jack called his wife in Seattle, who was away on business at an Academy of Management conference presenting a paper on Emotional Intelligence. Her response was not what he expected. "When do we make the plans for the move?" Jack did not know what to do at this point because he was very happy living in a high-rise in New York City overlooking Central Park. His daughter was in one of the best public schools in the city, mid-year of her eighth grade. Jack called his boss Maryann Victor, Senior Vice President of National Sales. "Maryann, I think HR wants to send me to Wisconsin." Mary replied, "I need a solid emerging-markets sales person in Wisconsin. Jack, you will have thirty people reporting to you and your region will be in the Northeast. You are in the driver's seat, it is your decision, your salary will go up by fifty percent and we will pay all relocation costs---including selling your apartment in Manhattan."

Jack did not know if this was a good time for him to move but also realized that finding another job at this point in his career may be challenging. He is already fifty-three and chances of him finding a suitable job in the financial industry may take some time. His position as Customer Relationship Manager is thriving with twenty people under him now and his salary is working out well for him at $180,000.

Despite his wife's enthusiasm to find the road to riches and enjoy the extra income, he was wondering about his daughter's school and his wife's job-search to be a professor---which is her life goal, and her Ph.D. was about to be approved at Yale University.

Coming up the Ranks

Jack's mother ran a German American delicatessen on 57th street for twenty years and she had a reputation that was the best when it came to both baking and catering; his father was a Mortgage Bond trader who developed the products with Lou Raneiri, a well-known Wall Street intrapreneur. Lou could take any mortgage and make it into a bond and trade it in open market. Success was imminent for Jack; from the time he was twelve, he sat on his father's lap while he traded bonds and spent the rest of the time at the deli making potato pancakes and bratwurst.

Jack's father was a great football player and had scholarships to Champlain University and Dartmouth but was called into World War II during the Army of Occupation. He saved four prisoners of war in a dungeon in Germany that he stumbled upon by accident. He was smoking a cigarette, the hot ash flew down the sewage grate, and he heard a loud scream from someone saying, "Ouch, help me!" He could not find his commander and all of his comrades were searching for German documents to collect war contraband and intelligence. He grabbed a crowbar and shimmered the grate open, threw a rope down and pulled each man up one at a time. They were frail, hungry, weak, and could hardly talk. He gave them water and whatever rations he had and waited for his commander to send help. Three helicopters came and took the soldiers to a German hospital. He received the Medal of Honor from President Truman. Jack's father always instilled in him a sense of leadership and helping people both above his level and above his followers to be the best they can be.

Jack was not as strong as his father in terms of football, but he was great at golf. He led teams of children from Bedford Stuyvesant in Brooklyn and created mentorships throughout the city of Manhattan and the surrounding suburbs.

Jack learned that he could develop leaders by using Situational Leadership created by Paul Hersey and Ken Blanchard. He knew when to push, when to pull back, and when to just let people strive on their own. He would use a telling style when people were new and needed a great deal of direction, pullback, and delegate when he knew the people had high skill levels. He also was aware of what he was good at and what he was not so great at and let others lead with their strengths.

Flying High in April Shot Down in May

Jack was working as a Bond Trader Assistant at Morgan Stanley right in the heart of the theater district when he got married. He interviewed with Merrill Lynch right before leaving on his honeymoon. While in Hawaii, he received a call from his recruiter. "Jack, they want you. Starting salary $105,000 with a $15,000 sign on bonus, want it?" "I'll take it!" Jack responded. Jack's wife was also excited since Jack was only making $80,000 at that time. Jack was laid off three months later as Merrill began to feel the pangs of Wall Street Bond Trading coming to a screeching halt after Collateralized Mortgage Bonds dropped in rating and Lou Ranerie's invention became unwound. The market flew to quality away from Mortgage Bonds and into the United States Government Bonds for safety. Jack remembers that time as daunting, being recently married, feeling a sense of success, and then turmoil. Luckily, for him, his boss Scott German gave him two months to search for a job. Jack hit the ground running with resumes all over the street. When he finally landed an interview, the recruiter said to him, "Jack, I am not sure if this is a good thing or not, but I received four resumes from you for this position." Jack assured her that it was a good thing and pure enthusiasm, but it was not. Jack sent resumes to everyone everywhere and sometimes could not keep track of how many were sent out in any given day. Although it was a challenging time for Jack and his wife, Jack felt that he had learned a great deal from the experience and perhaps would have been better off staying put at one of the best investment banks on the street. It was a very valuable lesson for him.

Jack said to himself, "There is something to be said about taking on risk, knowing what your value is at all times, and continuously developing yourself." At Morgan Stanley, Jack took sixty courses in one year, adding a ton of knowledge to his resume---upon joining his current firm.

"I remember my first day on the job at my firm. The human resource executive made his last presentation before retiring and it was so profound that I knew I was in the right place---I found a home." Jack got into the Sales and Trading training, which is only for the pedigree intellectuals. He learned more in six months than he had learned in two years of his MBA at Yale, where he met his wife. After two years of rotation through equities and bonds, Jack knew his passion was in the Mortgage Bond area. He was the top trader and began running the trading desk. After two years as the leader of the Bond Trading desk, he was asked to run the customer relationship management team and work on client acquisitions and customer satisfaction. He interacted regularly with the top brass of the firm and became well known as not only a revenue generator but also a people person that could convince any client into placing their confidence and trust in the investment bank.

A year later, Jack was promoted to director of customer relationship management. He learned what leaders did well and what they lacked. He zigged when he had to and zagged when he needed to. He never lost an opportunity to learn to develop his leadership skills.

Becoming a Managing Director

At age forty-seven, Jack was asked to lead his financial institution to a new level. He was in one of the worst performing units of the firm and he had to turn it around quickly. He used what he learned from two of his prior leaders Ellen Peterson and Kevin Roberts of Saatchi and Saatchi. Ellen was in the financial industry for years and made it to the top brass from hard work in the mortgage-trading desk as an intern during college. From there, she was asked to be an assistant mortgage bond trader and went to Harvard Business School. She used what is known in the academic and now corporate world as "Transformational Leadership." She developed a sense of urgency in her people to improve the business unit. Kevin, at the time when Jack met him, was the CEO of Saatchi and Saatchi. Kevin made a presentation at the Academy of Management annual meeting that changed Jack's perspective on leadership. Kevin taught Jack to be an inspirer---not just a leader. "It was happening so fast; there were so many great things said by Kevin. I took copious notes, and I could remember it all---it was as if he was speaking directly to me," Jack said to himself. One piece of Kevin's presentation stuck with Jack throughout his career and still does today. The key point Kevin told the participants was that he swapped command and control for unleash and inspire. Jack put this on a plaque in his office:

Inspiration unlocks human potential
Inspiration is non-coercive
Inspiration is non-hierarchical
Inspiration is viral and contagious
Inspiration builds to a tipping point
Beyond inspiration, there is magic
Inspiration takes you from mediocre performance through High Performance to Peak Performance.

While Kevin felt that being a Manager or even a Leader is just another label but stepping up to being an inspirer of Emotional Intelligence is what it takes to lead, Ellen agreed with Kevin but added another component. Ellen felt that in some cases, transactional leadership was necessary to get the team or group started on the right track. Ellen used transactional leadership only when necessary because she felt that it is like placing a carrot-on-a-stick approach to leadership. Jack noticed that a renowned scholar trained Ellen by the name of Bruce Avolio. She used Bruce's four components of leadership:

Idealized influence when aiming to develop a shared vision and improve relationships with followers

Individualized consideration when they would like to concentrate on identifying employees' individual needs and empower followers in order to build a learning climate and mobilize follower support toward the goals and objectives at the senior organizational level

Intellectual stimulation to propel knowledge sharing in the company to generate more innovative ideas and solutions for new and demanding issues that come up constantly in our hypercompetitive economic environment, and;

Inspirational motivation to focus on inspiring people and not just treat them as human assets. This sets a higher level of desired expectations for them.

Jack found that these four dimensions of transformational leadership represents how an effective leader working in today's knowledge-based economy could develop and manage intellectual capital in large corporations.

Jack was looking at leadership from a new perspective now as his career began to move one level up. Jack remembers his days living in a suburb of Manhattan, a small island called Staten Island. His father was a great leader and supported his basketball league as coach, cub scouts as Cub Scout leader, and the baseball coordinator of a new league in which his father and his friends' fathers were all coaches. Jack remembers his father to be jovial and likable but even he knew his limitations. When Jack was sad from dating breakups, his father encouraged him to have a chip on his shoulder and realize his value of being a good kid with high integrity, handsomeness, and strength. Never doubting Jack's ability, his father would encourage only the best from him. In some ways now, Jack looks back at his father as a transformational leader.

Reflecting on Jack's Motivation

"I am quick to make decisions and never look an opportunity with a shy eye," Jack always said about his motivations, and most of all, "I love to go beyond the status quo and do more and be more than my competitors." He learned this from a quote by Robert Iger, CEO of Walt Disney Corporation. Robert's quote was spot on.

Optimism is a very very important part of leadership. People don't like to follow pessimists. -Robert Iger

Jack had a plague in his office by L. P. Jacks that said:

A master in the art of living draws no sharp distinction between his work and his play; his labor and his leisure; his mind and his body; his education and his recreation. He hardly knows which is which. He simply pursues his vision of excellence through whatever he is doing, and leaves others to determine whether he is working or playing. To himself, he always appears to be doing both.

Jack did not only learn from his father; his mother was a true leader also. She would organize and manage her delicatessen like a whirlwind. She always built Jack's self-esteem and was his biggest cheerleader. She had certain traits that Jack remembered: Integrity, Intelligence, Drive, Energy, and the Ability to lead and inspire people. Traits became a way of life for Jack. Jack analyzed his bosses, his professors, his uncle Joe the lawyer, and his aunt Mickey who ran a crew of women to help the United States win the War by working hard in the states to prepare the soldiers. He even learned from his Aunt Maria who, in Italy, was a victim of the German occupation. She taught him perseverance and determination to hold on to the last crumb to survive. When she experienced things that happened and told Jack, tears came down her eyes and Jack wept. His uncle Reid Diggs once told him about the slaves that he had in Virginia. Reid mentioned that they took his name and were like family----he was a proud slave owner. Jack disagreed with him and felt that all men and women should be free, but Jack did remember the tear coming down from his uncle's eyes. Now, building his traits became an obsession for him. He accumulated as many as he could, and he attempted to master each of them one at a time for perhaps a week and then move onto another.

Jack told his daughter of a leader that once said:

"Be who...you were meant to be, and you will set the world on fire."

Jack also told his daughter that there is nothing that she cannot be or do and that all she has to do is go out and get it. He talked about entrepreneurship and what he experienced in his work, "Intrapreneurship." Then he said there is a term he uses in the boardroom to motivate his followers. His daughter asked, "What term is that, dad?" Jack answered, "I would like to introduce a new term today called 'Motrapreneur,'":

A Motrapreneur is someone who takes stock in themselves and sets up a personalized reward system for themselves, takes calculated risks, and is determined to stay on purpose by incremental improvement with the intention of creating a sense of intensity and direction coupled with a burning desire to live to their fullest potential.

Jack's daughter Nicolette wanted to be an actuary from a very young age and planned to go to Penn State where her grandmother went and became a finance executive at Macy's department store worldwide. She wanted to help people save for retirement and manage insurance policies for people so that they can retire and enjoy life and travel the world. Jack encouraged her even though he wanted her to follow him in his own footsteps. He realized that she may change her mind and join him on the trading desk, but he wanted her to have her own individuality and create her own destiny.

The Journey had Pitfalls

While holding a prominent executive position as profit-and-loss analyst, a trader he supported held back the coupon on mortgage bonds but paid the finance charge. Coupons are income while finance charges are expenses. The trader was hiding the profit to offset losses that he incurred while trading the bonds. Jack was faced with a seventeen-million-dollar deficit. His boss called him into the office and told him, "I am not going to be able to move you to the next level, Jack!" Jack failed early in his career, but he learned from the failure and even though he thought all this documentation had a trail to some sought of success, somehow he did not see it.

Another trader hid money in the pricing of the bonds and later was determined to overprice bonds that actually lost money. Seventeen million dollars had to be changed in the balance sheet after the annual report was printed. However, the audit trail was built on brick and mortar, and he was correct, realizing it was his account and that the trader hid the money under his watch. He made an accounting error, but he did not do anything illegal. The Security and Exchange Commission came down on him hard as his bosses attempted to place the blame on him. He was interviewed and told what to say by his firm appointed lawyer for him in a conference room. He had a Harvard lawyer back him up in the conversation and coach him. The trader just walked off the trading desk and left Jack holding the problem alone. His bosses, also in trouble, held Jack out to dry by placing blame on him instead of the trader. The Security and Exchange commissioner was angry and yelled at Jack in the conference room. Nevertheless, Jack stood his ground and told the SEC official that he followed the rules and that the trader hid the money in the value of the bonds in a way in which he could not account for them based on current market sales and liquidation. If nothing was sold in this particular bond market, the value is relative and could not be calculated precisely. Jack was so ashamed that he knew that his career at this investment bank may have come to a standstill. It did not, however, and he survived. What saved him was his positive nature and his frank appellation at what actually took place and not what he did wrong but what the trader was trying to hide to save his own career at Jack's expense.

Earlier in his career, when he first started out in profit and loss analysis, the person training him changed the cost price on the bonds in front of him. Jack told the person training him that he could not change cost prices on any financial assets because bonds are priced on a mark-to-market basis, but the person manipulated Jack to believe him. He had a convincing, aggressive personality and Jack did not know how to be assertive enough at this point in his career. However, behind the person's back, Jack wrote a letter to his immediate boss, but his boss decided to deflect on the memo and not address the issue---he also questioned Jack's integrity. Jack could not defend himself because he had a strong respect for authority figures since his childhood. Three weeks later, the senior boss along with a crew of people came to realize that bonds might not be priced correctly. They found twenty-four million in losses in his account due to the paper trail of changing the cost of the bonds. When Jack's senior boss found out about it, he challenged Jack and looked at his work but realized that Jack had high integrity----the letter sent to his senior boss saved his career. His immediate boss was driving on a highway several states away when he heard the news and almost drove off the road. Jack blew the whistle, and the person was fired but that also left him feeling that not everyone is honest and has personal integrity. However, Jack realized that this was his faith and righteousness was his rock and he would never let someone manipulate him again like that.

Jack's Decision

Was Jack prepared for this new career to move one level up in Wisconsin? It was a pivotal move. One that could make or break his career. His wife was on board. He remembered the Peter Principle by Laurence Peters that said that all leaders rise to an occasion in which they fail. He did not want to fail.

The Wisconsin job would put him in charge of a larger span of control, double his salary, and help him prepare his daughter for her college years at an Ivy League school of her choice.

Jack heard that the word on the street is that if he took it, he was a success, but if he did not, he might as well remain a vice president for the rest of his life.

Jack knew his wife can find work anywhere, but what if her Ph.D. lands her a job at Yale, her alma mater or Harvard. Then what?

On the other hand, the new opportunity was a milestone to reflect on his success thus far. He had both depth and breadth now of the mortgage-backed security market and his clients loved him. This job was tempting and turning it down may make him look in mobilized and land-locked to New York City. Jack's boss Maryann texted him, "Jack, I know 24 hours is a short period of time, but I need your decision, or I am going with Tameka Watson. I want you to know that we still need a strong VP here if you decide not to go---your choice!" Tameka worked right next to Jack in the equities department; she did not know very much about mortgage bonds, but Maryann knew a good manager would pick up the skill set quickly and hit the ground running. Jack had a tough choice to make. Tameka was very competitive; she graduated from Harvard Business School with an MBA in finance, she was single, mobile, and would take the opportunity in a flash. She graduated top in her class in the Sales and Training program at the Investment Bank. Her mother was Secretary of State in the United States capital, and her father was in the Senator for the State of Illinois.

As Jack looked at his daughter studying in the dining room with her music on, his thoughts raced across his mind. He just wanted his wife to come back from Seattle and give him a big bear hug. "Perhaps I will hug all both of them together, and include my Maltese dog Buddy," Jack thought.

Discussion Questions:

1. How effective has Jackson Breaks been in his leadership before he got this new assignment?
2. Is he a transformational or transactional leader?
3. Does he have the necessary traits to lead? If so, what are they? If not, why not and what is he missing?
4. How may Jack use Situational Leadership if he takes the assignment?
5. To what extent is he leading a life that includes balance of both work and play?
6. Should he give up his life in the great city of Manhattan for one in which he will be challenged in the great city of Wisconsin?
7. If he does go, what about his wife's career placement as a tenured professor, and most importantly, about his daughter's school?
8. Has Jack ever failed? If so, how did he handle his failure? Did you ever fail? If yes, how? If not, why not?

Michael Provitera is a Management Trainer and Associate Professor of Organizational Behavior at

Barry University in Miami, Florida USA. He prepared this case based on fictitious information and some actual events that took place in his fifteen-year career as an executive in the financial industry. The case is unique for leadership and management discussion learning as the basis of classroom [or training] discussion at both the graduate and undergraduate level [and executive seminars] rather than to illustrate either effective or ineffective handling of an administrative or personal career or leadership situation. The case is based on leadership ideas and creative assumptions made without reference or permission of the people named [all names are made up unless otherwise stated]. For further information regarding this case or for permission to use it in the classroom or for corporate training, contact the author, Dr. Michael Provitera, at docprov@msn.com or visit the author's website at http://docprov.com.

The Last Castle Video Case: Applying Leadership Theory

Dr. Michael J. Provitera, Management Consultant, Business Book Author, Management Professor

Published 9-11-2018 (All Rights Reserved)

Copyright ®Dr. Michael J. Provitera September 11, 2018

Case Overview

The Last Castle tells a story about a three-star general, Eugene Irwin, who is sent to prison under the command of a ruthless prison warden, Colonel Winter. Its central story takes place in an old castle that was renovated into a prison. The castle has a small wall that Colonel Winter allows the prisoners to rebuild. The wall symbolizes Colonel Winter's leadership (formal leader). When prisoner Irwin begins to build himself an army, the prisoners then knock down the wall only to rebuild it under their new leadership (informal leader). In its simplest interpretation, the movie provides a leadership question: Are leaders born or could anybody be made into a leader? At a much deeper level, the movie asks what decisions we, as leaders, are willing to make for a cause that we believe is right.

Specific Teaching Objectives

You will learn to apply leadership theory to your careers and personal lives using leadership examples from the film *The Last Castle* (DreamWorks Pictures, 2001). The characters and situations that take place throughout the movie provide examples of leaders and followers in action. Three main leadership theories will be explored:

- Trait Theory (Stogdill, 1948:1974; Kirkpatrick and Locke, 1991)
- Situational Leadership® (Hersey and Blanchard, 1969)
- Charismatic Leadership (House, 1977; Conger and Kanungo, 1987; Nadler and Tushman, 1989), Transformational Leadership Theory (Duluga, 1988; Podsadoff, MacKenzie, Moorman, and Fetter, 1990; Burns, 1978; Bass, 1985:1990; Bass, Avolio, Goodheim, 1987), and Transactional Leadership (Pawar and Eastman, 1997).

Charismatic, Transformational, and Transactional leadership are all considered one.

Each theory can be taught using different scenes in the film, but the whole film covers the gamut of the leadership theories to be explained above. Other theories can be substituted at the instructor's discretion or students may also wish to apply other theories as a form of discussion.

Discussion Questions

1. First, watch the entire movie with one intermission if time allows (the Preferred intermission would be directly after Aguilar gets shot). Are the traits that Prisoner Irwin

(Robert Redford) display as a leader in the film The Last Castle consistent with those identified by the trait model of leadership (Stogdill, 1974)?

a. What are the traits that prisoner Irwin show?
b. Could you link one trait with one leader in any one scene? If so, explain.
c. How can you use trait theory in your professional and personal life?

2. Review the scenes of prisoner Irwin and Yates. The first is when Yates introduces himself and tells Irwin who his father was. In addition, review the relationship with Aguilar and prisoner Irwin, and the Sergeant Major and prisoner Irwin.

a. What overall style of leadership does each leader (Winter and Irwin) use and what is the readiness level of the followers at any given time in the movie (just choose one leadership style and readiness level for each leader)?

b. Has prisoner Irwin exemplified the situational leadership style model of leadership? Has he used different styles of leadership for each different follower-leader relationship:
- Telling (Provide specific instructions and closely supervise performance)
- Selling (Explain decisions and provide opportunity for clarification)
- Participating (Share ideas and facilitate in making decisions)

- Delegating (Turn over responsibility for decisions and implementation)

Each story can be taught using a different part of the film. The key is to learn how prisoner Irwin uses his leadership styles appropriately.

c. What applications can you make to your career as a manager, the subordinates you lead, or other situations in your personal and professional life?

3. Review the scenes in which prisoner Irwin leads his followers. Several scenes throughout the movie exemplify leadership decisions and articulation.

a. Has prisoner Irwin exemplified the following leadership styles? Explain.
- Charismatic Leadership
- Transformational leadership

b. Which leader is more of a transactional versus transformational leader? Explain.

c. What applications of the leadership theory exemplified in this case study can you make to your career as a manager, the subordinates you lead, or other situations in your personal and professional life?

References

Tracy, J. B., and Hinkin, T. R. (1998, September). Transformational leadership or effective managerial practices? Groups and Organizational Management. Thousand Oaks, CA: Sage. 23 (3): 220.

Bass, B. M. (1985). Leadership and performance beyond expectation. New York Press Publishers: New York.

Bass, B. M. (1990). From transactional to transformational leadership: Learning to share the vision.

Bass, B. M., Avolio, B. J., and Goodheim, L. (1987). Biography and assessment of transformational leadership at the world class level. Journal of Management, 13: 7-19.

Stogdill, R. M. (1948, January). Personal factors associated with leadership: A survey of the literature," Journal of Psychology, 25: 35-64.

Stogdill, R. M. (1974). Handbook of Leadership. New York: Free Press.

Gibb, C. A. (1954). Leadership. In Handbook of Social Psychology, ed. Gardner Lindzey (Reading, MA: Addison-Wesley.

Jenning, E. E. (1964, Autumn). The Anatomy of Leadership, Management of Personnel Quarterly, 1.

Crom, J. O. (1990, January), "What's new in leadership," Executive Excellence, 7: 15-16.

Kirkpatrick, S. A. and Locke, E. A. (1991). Leadership: Do traits matter? Academy of Management Executive 5 (2):44-57.

Coleman, D. (1998). What makes a leader? Harvard Business Review, 76 (6): 93-102.

Hersey, P. and Blanchard, K. (1996). Management of Organizational Behavior: Utilizing Human Resources, 7th ed. Englewood Cliffs, NJ: Prentice Hall.

Hersey, P. and Blanchard, K. (1996). "Great ideas revisited: Revisiting the life-cycle theory of leadership," Training and Development, 50 (1):42-47.

House (1977). Theory of Charismatic Leadership

Conger and Kanungo, (1987). Toward a Behavioral Theory of Charismatic Leadership in Organizational Settings

Duluga, (1988). Relationship of Transformational and Transactional Leadership with Employee Influencing Strategies

Podsadoff, MacKenzie, Moorman, and Fetter, (1990). Transformational Leader Behaviors and Their Effects on Followers' Trust in Leader, Satisfaction, and Organizational Citizenship Behaviors.

Pawar, B. S., and Eastman, K. K. (1997). The nature and implications of contextual influences on transformational leadership: A conceptual examination. Academy of Management Review, 22: 80-99.

Managing People

Managing People

Teaching Leadership using the film *"Facing the Giants"*

Dr. Michael J. Provitera, Management Consultant, Business Book Author, Management Professor

Published 9-11-2018 (All Rights Reserved)

Copyright ®Dr. Michael J. Provitera September 11, 2018

Abstract

Leading people can be challenging with all the theories and models of leadership available to executives today. This case study suggests the film *Facing the Giants* (2006) as an effective way to introduce management to the study of leadership. A leadership model is introduced to participants and then a movie is shown in its entirety. When the film is over, a discussion-learning session is conducted. The discussion-learning approach is used to help participants discover the application of a leadership model coupled with the rationale of analyzing leadership styles used in the film. The case study begins with a general discussion of the use of film in management education, introduces a method of application of leadership theory, and explores various scenes and how the leadership model can be applied to some of the scenes in the film. Then, discussion questions for spirituality and leadership are provided to help facilitate discussion-learning after the movie is shown. In addition to the discussion format, a questionnaire is used after watching the movie to engage participants in an open-ended discussion. This case-study presents both the discussion questions and the survey questions. The leadership seminars that were conducted indicated that participants found the movie to be entertaining and an enjoyable experience. Participants also provided feedback that showed a perceived application of the leadership model and how to apply the leadership model in the workplace.

Keywords: leadership, management, spirituality, motion pictures in management education

Introduction

Teaching leadership can be challenging given followers' conceptualization of the practice of leadership (Hay and Hodgkinson, 2006) coupled with effectively teaching basic and advanced business concepts in the 21st century (Parker, 2009). Students majoring in business often have negative attitudes toward the demanding work hours necessary to be successful as leaders (Fry and Cohen, 2008). This has changed in many sectors of business as real-estate and flextime are being introduced. However, many universities are providing lectures online, in-class, and a combination of both for one course in the same semester to meet the unique needs of students today. In light of these concerns, the film *Facing the Giants* (2006) aids in the advancement of participants' understanding of leadership, ethics, and spirituality as it highlights the tactics leaders employ during difficult situations. Also, the case study illustrates some of the reasons why people may resist change and stimulates a discussion of some of the challenges facing leaders today.

Using film to demonstrate concepts in leadership is often used in management education, and a significant body of research exists supporting the use of film as a powerful medium for providing examples of the application of theory, presenting management models and concepts, and facilitating discussion learning (Champoux, 1999, 2001, 2007; Billsberry and Gilbert, 2008).

Leaders today have grown up with the Internet, video games, television, and movies as central parts of their lives and therefore expect the utilization of technology when learning (Parker, 2009). Therefore, entertaining participants becomes increasingly important along with effectively teaching basic and advanced business concepts in the 21st century. Stimulating new attitudes about the subject matter (Hobbs, 1998) and demonstrating the relevance of a topic to a participant's life or work (Oishi, 2007) may further engage students. Moreover, Tejeda (2008) found that film is like no other medium in its ability to focus participants' attention on the behavioral aspects of people and the situations that they face. In addition, the images and emotional content of film are likely to improve the retention of training material and how leadership may be applied to the real-world (Champoux, 1999). Participants may remember the experience when the learning mode stimulates emotions that may not be readily available in a typical discussion about the subject matter. This particular movie has many scenes that draw upon emotional underpinnings that relate to both people's lives and professions.

Film use in the classroom has many applications as a teaching resource that may appeal to the learner's imagination and encourage critical thinking (Billsberry & Gilbert, 2008; Champoux, 2001); and the social realism of drama can help illustrate concepts and thus facilitate learning (Billsberry & Gilbert, 2008; Bumpus, 2005; Champoux, 2001). In an anonymous (2007) review in a leading journal, scholars capture the essence of using film in the classroom:

Video-based material in all formats lightens the preparatory workload, quickens the cadence of learning, heightens the immediacy of the experience for those who are participating in the conversation, and makes tangible both the experience and the message that we wish to convey. Moreover, videos also play directly in our mental cinemas, and, in doing so, open up a world of unlimited possible connections on which to build effective managerial conversations.

Thus, films are a useful and inexpensive teaching medium for presenting longitudinal views of leaders and decisions in context, portraying leadership artistry and morality, and illustrating leaders' beliefs, values, and, most importantly, their actions (English and Steffy, 1997, p.107). A leadership case study using a Hollywood-type feature film can offer participants a chance to ponder on what they learned while watching the movie and compare and contrast it with leadership theory that they may already be aware of, may be currently applying in the workplace, or may be in the process or learning.

The Facing the Giants Film

The film is about a Christian high school football coach who uses his undying faith to battle the giants (which happens to be the name of the opposing team and becomes a metaphor for dealing with obstacles in life). The movie captures how a coach and team players face fear and failure. Many critics favored the movie as an indication of the leadership component coupled with spirituality. A few of their comments are indicative below.

Reeves (2006) contends that Facing the Giants is a great movie about how God can change lives on and off the football field. Every family in America should see it. While White (2006) stated that his wife and I laughed and cried throughout this terrific movie. We were on the edge of our seats. Another critic by the name of Olson (2006), felt that the movie shows kids how to compete as a Christian athlete. It shows coaches how to integrate faith into their coaching. Moreover, it speaks to the unique relationship between coaches, players, and parents. A third critic by the name of Carter (2006) exclaimed that the movie is interwoven in a powerfully entertaining sports movie and that it is a life-transforming message. Everyone is overwhelmed by problems at times, and desperate to find real purpose and meaning in life.

In summary, the motion picture *"Facing the Giants"* (2006), can be used by management trainers and educators to introduce participants to the study of leadership coupled with a notion of spirituality. Participants do not have to be Christian to watch this film and the discussion about the topics, after viewing it, do not have to be related to Christianity. For example, a scholar by the name of Dr. Stephen Sussman, a professor of public administration at a university in Miami, Florida, provides a wide array of accolades on how the Jewish faith has called upon leaders throughout centuries to make an impact on the masses by doing right to others and helping the least among us. Thus, the key is to engage participants in the discussion of leadership and to include all faiths and spiritual practices in the discussion.

Watching the film can also generate a discussion about how spirituality adds a different, but effective, dimension to influencing followers. For example, in one scene, the coach tells the football player conducting a football crawl, sometimes referred as the "death crawl," with a man on his back, that he has been gifted with leadership capability and it is his right to use it. This notion may plant a seed in the participant's motivational mindset (see Mastering Self-Motivation, written by Dr. Michael J. Provitera) to accomplish a task that they have been wanting to finish or proceed in a direction in which they may have thought would be too challenging. Carpenter (2006) proclaimed that the leader in the movie playing the coach dares to challenge his players to believe that God can do the impossible on and off the football field. When faced with the unbelievable odds, the football team (named the Eagles) must step up to their greatest test of strength and courage.

Incorporating the film, Facing the Giants (2006), into the study of leadership provides an opportunity for participants to identify with issues and concepts that they may not have personally experienced and may increase their understanding of the relevance of spirituality and its possible impact on their day-to-day decision making. The following section provides a method of use of the movie for teaching a leadership model using what is known as "Discussion Learning."

Implementing the Discussion-learning Approach

Facing the Giants (2006) can be used for executive training or in leadership and management. Another suggested use of the case-study is an organizational behavior class at both the undergraduate and graduate level.

The first thing that should be done before the movie is shown, whether shown in part or in its entirety, is to provide an understanding of leadership theory. Many models and theories can be used for this process. Once a conceptualization of the leadership model or theory is introduced and the participants understand it thoroughly, then the movie should be viewed in its entirety with one intermission about half way through (suggested break after the player makes amends with his father in his architectural business office).

Once the movie is over, begin the class discussion about the movie in an open forum. At this time, participants are fully engaged and ready to discuss the film. After an open forum type discussion, the discussion questions can be addressed. The open forum enables students to say whatever comes to their mind without prompting them to answer a question. The discussion questions, on the other hand, are contrived to elicit circumstances in which the participants had experience either being part of or observing a leader in action or the application of a film to some sort of theory or practice.

Another method of use would be to have the participants write about the movie in the form of a reflection paper (see appendix B). This option gives participants the time to ponder on their own about how the leadership model can be applied to the scenes of the movie, going back to the leadership model or theory discussed prior to showing the film. This individual reflection coupled with the film encourages them to review leadership theory so that they can apply it to their workplace.

It is important to note that time constraints, technology and copyright provisions may limit viewing options (Billsberry & Gilbert, 2008); however, the film should be viewed in its totality during training if possible, in one sitting with one intermission. As long as no consulting fee is ascertained or the audience is not being charged to watch the movie, then copyright issues should not be a problem (consult your copyright attorney regarding this matter to ensure that no unlawful action issues may transpire).

For trainers that purchase the movie and provide it as a mechanism of learning and developing leadership, permission should be granted by the producers (see Dr. Provitera's case study found in this book titled "The Last Castle"). The movie may be used in its entirety or in individual scenes followed by discussions. Management educators, on the other hand, conducting fifty-minute classes can utilize a three-part viewing of the film using the parts proposed below. There will be some time remaining in each class to draw attention to important aspects of the story of the film in preparation for the final class discussion. The film can be divided as follows (the scene numbers are based on the commercially available DVD):

Part 1: Scenes 1–8 (approximately 33 minutes); the opening scene with the loosing game, the disappointed coach, players, and fans, the supporting wife

Part 2: Scenes 9–15 (approximately 47 minutes); revival, finding God in day-to-day decision making, finding faith through an unexpected visitor

Part 3: Scenes 16–28 (approximately 42 minutes); unleashed, facing reality, planning for good things to happen, hoping for overwhelming success in all aspects of life

The post-viewing discussion is based on the theory or model of leadership used coupled with the scenes from the movie. A list of discussion questions provides both trainers and management educators the option of full-class discussion or discussion in groups of four to six students by having one member of the group report their group's collective answers to the class as a whole. The following discussion questions can be used to facilitate the training discussion:

Discussion Questions on Spirituality

a. Has there ever been a time in your life that you recall in which you felt that some type of universal power intervened for you that led to success in your life or someone around you?
b. Compare and contrast the football team before and after they began to become more spiritual.
c. How has your faith in your spiritual life affected you in your life, in your parent's or grandparent's life, or your friend's life? Is there any scenario that took place in the scenes of this movie that can be useful to you going forward? If so, explain. If not, why not?

Applying Leadership Theory

There are many leadership theories that could be applied to the film and a trainer or professor may want to use one in which they are familiar with. For this case-study, situational leadership is the preferred leadership model. Paul Hersey (1996) created the Situational Leadership Model and is an expert in human behavior and behavioral management. The situational leadership model views leaders as varying their emphasis on task and relationship behaviors to best deal with different levels of follower maturity (Hersey, 1984).

Managers using the situational model must be able to implement the alternative leadership styles as needed. To do this, they have to understand the maturity level of followers in terms of their readiness for task performance. Once this step is done, they can then use the leadership style that best fits the situation, ergo, Situational-Leadership (Schermerhorn, 2010). Thus, a three-step model exists: determining the task, assessing readiness levels of followers, and picking a leadership style.

The coach in the film *Facing the Giants* had to determine the task and readiness-level for the team as a whole as well as some of the individual players. Determining the readiness level of a group of people is more difficult and more challenging than when readiness-determination is made for each person individually. However, this type of application of the model provides a pedagogical and anagogical exercise that helps students learn how to affectively lead groups of people all at the same time.

Questions that transpire when using the situational-leadership model are: What was the task for the players (individually, or as a group), what was the readiness level of the followers (R1, R2, R3, R4), and what was the leadership style (S1, S2, S3, S4) used by the coach. This analysis can be determined for specific scenes. Participants are then asked to provide a synopsis of specific scenes in their analysis indicating the specific task(s), the readiness level of the follower(s), and the leadership style selected by the coach. The best way to accomplish this is to have participants illustrate their example using the situational leadership model. The questions below may be used as a guide.

a. How did the coach assess the readiness level of the players (either as a group, or individually)? What were the specific readiness levels for particular scenes for each of the three parts of the movie? Provide a synopsis of specific scenes in your analysis as they relate to the readiness level of the followers. Keep the task in mind since that is the first step in the Situational Leadership Model application.

b. What situational style of leadership has the coach exemplified in specific scenes that you found in each of the parts of the movie? Provide a summary of the style(s) of leadership used below, detailed by Paul Hersey and his Situational Leadership Model:

- Telling (provide specific instructions and closely supervise performance)
- Selling (explain decisions and provide opportunity for clarification
- Participating (share ideas and facilitate in making decisions)
- Delegating (turn over responsibility for decisions and implementation)

Provide a brief synopsis of how the leader in the movie exemplified each of the four styles, or any one leadership style in a particular scene of leadership coupled with the specific task and the readiness level of the followers. Illustrate your work using the Situational Leadership Model (Hersey and Blanchard, 1996). For example: The task is the death crawl, the readiness level is readiness level three (Able, unwilling, and insecure), and the leader selected leadership style is three (participating).

c. What applications of the movie coupled with the Situational Leadership Model can you use in your career as a manager, with the subordinates you lead, or with other situations in your personal and professional life? Illustrate your examples using the situational leadership model.

Methodology

The survey questions are available for use, with some minor alterations. The survey suggested for an empirical study is adopted from Parker (2009, p.135). A copy of the survey items can be found in Appendix A at the end of this article. The survey was not administered for the development of this case-study. The results of selected voluntary comments after a brief training discussion following the viewing of the movie (or selected scenes) by the respondents are detailed below.

Findings

Some comments regarding the usefulness of the film in enhancing management education and training are worth stating. Below are five selected comments that participants wrote down and discussed in a training session in the discussion learning component of the session. This is not an empirical study and participants were asked if their comments can be presented publicly in an anonymous manner. They all agreed.

"It was an excellent movie, thank you for bringing it to our attention."

"After watching the scenes of the movie and illustrating the leadership model, things began to become much clearer to me."

"Movies make training time more fun and enjoyable."

"I enjoyed watching Facing the Giants and I will show this movie to my family."

"After watching the movie, I told my family about it and my daughter who is nine years old told me that she watched it in school, and she then told me that she promised to give her all at everything that she does. This changed the dialogue around the house to be more positive when it came to challenges and opportunities in life."

Discussion

Using the *Facing the Giants* film in the classroom has merit. The film *Facing the Giants* offers a fresh appellation of how a low-budget film and has reached so many venues. Films such as this one provides leadership scenarios coupled with spiritual virtues that some people can relate to.

Paul Hersey, and the Center for Leadership Studies formerly in Escondido, California, continue to strive in teaching and training situational leaders. Here is a note from the website situational.com:

For more than 45 years, The Center for Leadership Studies, founded by Dr. Paul Hersey, has been the global home of the original Situational Leadership® Model. With over 14 million leaders trained, Situational Leadership® is the most successful and widely adopted leadership model available. Deployed in more than 70% of Fortune 500 companies, our Situational Leadership® Model and influence-focused courses enable leaders to engage in effective performance conversations that build trust, increase productivity and drive behavior change. CLS services customers both domestically and internationally through an extensive network comprised of over 200 learning professionals in more than 25 languages.

Hersey (2010) argues that the next situational leader will need to get more done with less and they will need to do this more quickly. Providing participants with an introduction and application of this model offers a pedagogical and anagogical exercise in the real-world application of leadership.

Implications for Management

Managers can use this case study to implement a brief leadership training overview as an introduction to a broader leadership training platform that can expand to a more professional level at the Center for Leadership Studies or with other leadership training vendors if a different model of leadership is utilized.

Employees with leadership potential can be selected to go through the proposed leadership exercise that is provided in this case study as an indication of their role as future leaders of the organization. By beginning the dialogue of the situational leadership model, or whatever model that the professor or trainer would like to use, discussion learning, and the *Facing the Giants* movie can offer an entertaining and enlightening experience for managerial implication.

Limitations

First and foremost, only one leadership model has been applied in this leadership training and development case-study approach. While the option is open to use other models, this case does not make an attempt to show how another models can be used and only suggests that it may be possible. Moreover, there is little empirical research supporting the Situational Leadership model, but the basic use of the model has merit in the corporate environment. Graeff (1983) contends that leaders might do well to consider altering styles to achieve the best fits with followers' situations.

An important note to consider is that more specific research in the area of using film in training leaders is much needed.

Directions for Future Research

This case-study can be used in its whole or in part. The scenes from the movie have been used in training sessions in high-schools, elementary schools, college classrooms, and executive trainings. The case-study is designed for in-class, training rooms, and online learning. Permission to use this case-study from the author's standpoint is granted, any unofficial use barring copyright is the sole responsibility of the user and full discretion is on them. The movie rights will always remain with the producers and users of this case-study can feel free to reach out to them to inquire about the movie. Feel free to contact the author at docprov.com anytime to discuss your experience using this case study.

It would be interesting to see the results of an empirical study whereby participants in different sections of the same training are tested on the same material where one group serves as a control group and a second group is used as an experimental group. One group watches the movie without the prior training on the leadership model while the other has the formal leadership training.

Questions for future training enhancement may be: How much knowledge can be ascertained in simply learning the model and applying it in a class case-study format as opposed to watching a movie and applying the model to specific scenes? What would be the responses to the spirituality questions with the group that did not watch the movie versus the group that did? Trainers and management professors should continue to conduct empirical research on how the use of films in training sessions or classrooms (online or in brick-and-mortar formats) can be used for teaching or enhancing leadership among participants.

Conclusion

Using the situational-leadership model coupled with discussion learning is at the heart of this case study.

The film *Facing the Giants* (2006) and the discussion-learning exercise has been used in undergraduate and graduate courses along with the training and development of executives. Participants have indicated that the film and the following discussion-learning exercise helped them to analyze and apply the Situational Leadership Model (Hersey and

Blanchard, 1996). While this model was selected as the model of choice, other models, such as but not limited to, transformational leadership or path-goal theory could also have been used either individually or collectively. Each theory can be taught using different scenes in the film.

Participants found the movie to be entertaining, emotionally moving, and applicable to their day-to-day life challenges. They enjoyed analyzing and writing about the movie in the form of a film reflection, they expressed gratitude that the movie was brought to their attention, and they felt that they would like to share the movie with others. Therefore, using film in training and development, classroom lectures, or online-learning engages participants to be better equipped as leaders.

References

Anonymous, (2007). "Book Review: 'Out of this World' High-Performing Teams, A Video Tour" Academy of Management Learning & Education, 6 (3): 412.

Billsberry, J., & Gilbert, L. (2008). Using Ronald Dahl's Charlie and the Chocolate Factory to teach different recruitment and selection paradigms. Journal of Management Education, 32(2), 228-247.

Bumpus, M. A. (2005). Using motion pictures to teach management: Refocusing the camera lens through the infusion approach to diversity. Journal of Management Education, 29(6), 792-815.

Carpenter, E. L. (2006). Facing the Giants Movie Review Dove Family-Approved. Found on website http://www.dove.org/reviewpopup.asp?Unique_ID=5672 on January 1, 2010.

Champoux, J. E. (2007). Our feature presentation: Human resource management. Mason, OH: Thomson Higher Education.

Champoux, J. E. (2001). Animated films as a teaching resource. Journal of Management Education, 25(1), 79-100.

Champoux, J. E. (1999). Film as a teaching resource. Journal of Management Inquiry, 8(2), 206.

English, F. W., and Steffy, B. E. (1997). "Using Film to Teach Leadership in Educational Administration," Educational Administration Quarterly, 33 (1): 107-115.

Fry. L. W., and Cohen, M. P. (2009). "Spiritual Leadership as a Paradigm for Organizational Transformation and Recovery from Extended Work Hours Cultures," Journal of Business Ethics, 84: 265-274.

Graeff, C. L. (1983). "The Situational Leadership Theory: A Critical View," Academy of Management Review, 8: 285-291.

Hay, A. and Hodgkinson, M. (2006). Rethinking leadership: a way forward for teaching leadership? Leadership & Organization Development Journal, 27 (2): 144-158.

Hersey, P. (2010). Found on website http://www.situational.com/ on August 23, 2010.

Hersey, P. (1984). *The Situational Leader, Escondido, California: Center for Leadership Studies.*

Hersey, P. and Blanchard, K. (1996). *Management of organizational behavior: Utilizing human resources, 7th ed.* Englewood Cliffs, NJ: Prentice Hall.

Hobbs, R. (1998). Teaching with and about film and television: Integrating media literacy concepts into management education. Journal of Management Development, 17(4), 259-272.

Kendrick, A. (2006). *Facing the Giants.* Directed by Alex Kendrick with the supporting cast composed of volunteers from Sherwood Baptist Church, Albany, Georgia.

Oishi, L. (2007). Did you just see that? Online video sites can jumpstart lessons. Technology & Learning, 27(6), 32.

Parker, R. D. (2009). "Watch this Clip: Using Film as an Augmentation to Lecture and Class Discussion," Academy of Educational Leadership Journal, 13 (4): 129-135.

Provitera, M. J. (2007). The Last Castle Video Case Study: Applying Leadership Theory, The Management Case Study Journal, 7 (1): 1-5.

Provitera, M. J. (2011). *Mastering Self-Motivation: Preparing Yourself for Personal Excellence.* BusinessExpertPress publications.

Tejeda, M. (2008). A resource review for diversity film media. Academy of Management Learning & Education, 7(3), 434-439.

Schermerhorn, J. R. (2010). Found on website http://higheredbcs.wiley.com/legacy/college/schermerhorn/0471734608/module16/module16.pdf On August 2,

2010.

Sony Pictures Home Entertainment Inc., Facing the Giants. Found at website http://www.facingthegiants.com/about_quotes.php On December 27, 2009

Sussman, Stephen (2018). Personal contact interview via email at the Barry University, Miami, USA campus on September 11, 2018.

APPENDIX A: Survey Items for Further Discussion

　　　Survey items 1, 3, 4, 8, 10, and 11 deal with the relationship between the films shown in class and the leadership model presented in the training discussion, survey items 2 & 9 deal with participant enjoyment of watching films in general, and survey items 5, 6, 7 related to the participant's opinion of the professor and the course.

1) The films shown in class were helpful in illustrating topics covered in course material.

2) I like watching movies.

3) After watching the movies in class, I was better able to understand the concepts discussed in the texts.

4) Movies make the material more enjoyable to study.

5) I recommended this class to a friend in part because we watched movies during the course.

6) I would be likely to take this instructor again if there were movies shown in other classes.

7) I would be likely to take this instructor again if there were NO movies shown in other classes.

8) The movies shown in class reflected the material discussed.

9) I don't watch many films.

10) Showing movies in class was a complete waste of time.

11) The movies shown had little or nothing to do with the course material.

Focus Group Question

Please take a moment out to present your comment below in your own words. Writing your comment gives the trainer the right to use your quote when presenting the results of this exercise. Please include your name but be assured that complete anonymity will be kept with the highest integrity.

APPENDIX B: Film Reflection

Step 1 – Watch the Facing the Giants Video

Step 2 – Look for Management issues, theories, and models, or any other leadership topic.

Step 3 – Write a one-page (double-spaced sentenced with a 12-point font) review paper about the movie. Feel free to write more than one page if you would like to.

Step 4 – Add a quote from a leadership article that

comes from leadership and management theory or models such as Situational Leadership, Path-Goal Theory, Transformational Leadership, or McGregor's theory X and Y (things like empowerment and benefits are not theories or models).

Step 5 – Add a reference at the end of your paper that the quote came from. An example of this will be the title of your textbook, the authors, the publisher, and the page it came from (the reference should be on the second page if you write one page and the last page if you write more than one page. The page should be titled REFERENCES.

Step 6 – Attempt to relate the theory you choose with a scene in the movie by applying it to scenarios or undercurrents, conflicts, and tensions. One way of doing this is looking at the whole picture and then relating this to the theory. The main characters in the story are all attempting to work together but what is holding them back. Is it money, networks, working conditions, supervision, or anything else? What is the problem? Why is this person being held back and how does he or she break through oppression? Use a model or theory to explain the answer to these questions. Illustrate your use of the model or theory in pencil or pen when appropriate (typing the model in your illustration is also accepted).

Step 7 – Attempt to apply what you have learned to your career, work life, or personal life. How does management and spirituality come together for you and the people that you encounter on a day-to-day basis, read about, or learn from?

Managing People

Managing People

Selected Article Highlights from Harvard Business Review

On September 5, 2015, an online seminar titled "5 Essential Communications Skills to Catapult Your Career" by communications expert Kristi Hedges teaches aspiring executives five must-have communication skills: creating an intentional presence; being able to get buy-in; delivering executive briefings; connecting with distributed teams through virtual leadership; and giving and receiving direct feedback.

On April 30, 2009, John Baldoni, in his article titled "Five Ways to Sharpen Your Communication Skills," provides those ways below:

1. Know the fundamentals. Express yourself well verbally, as well as on paper or through email.

2. Think clearly about what you will say. Too many managers….*sketch* out thoughts rather than *flesh* them out.

3. Prepare for meetings. So often meetings go off track before they begin because managers and employees do not take the time to think about what they will say before they say it.

4. Engage in discussion. All too often, either due to the press of time or perhaps a feeling of over-importance, executives do not make it clear that they want to hear alternate points of view.

5. Listen to others. Discussions are meaningless if no one is listening.

In April 2, 2018, "10 Must Reads on Communication (with

featured article "The Necessary Art of Persuasion," by Jay A. Conger) in Paperback" by the Harvard Business Review, Robert B. Cialdini, Nick Morgan, and Deborah Tannen provides the insights and advice you need to:

- Pitch your brilliant idea—successfully
- Connect with your audience
- Establish credibility
- Inspire others to carry out your vision
- Adapt to stakeholders' decision-making style
- Frame goals around common interests
- Build consensus and win support.

Boris Groysberg and Michael Slind from the June 2012 Harvard Business Review issue titled "Leadership is a Conversation," state that:

The command-and-control approach to management has in recent years become less and less viable. Globalization, new technologies, and changes in how companies create value and interact with customers have sharply reduced the efficacy of a purely directive, top-down model of leadership. What will take the place of that model? Part of the answer lies in how leaders manage communication within their organizations—that is, how they handle the flow of information to, from, and among their employees. Traditional corporate communication must give way to a process that is more dynamic and more sophisticated. Most important, that process must be conversational.

Scott Edinger, in his Harvard Business Review article titled "Three Elements of Great Communication, According to Aristotle," published on January 17, 2013, states that:

In my nearly 20 years of work in organization development, I've never heard anyone say that a leader communicated too much or too well. On the contrary, the most common improvement suggestion I've seen offered up on the thousands of 360 [degree] evaluations [those that tap the knowledge of many people around you when conducting an annual personnel review] I've reviewed over the years is that it would be better if the subject in question learned to communicate more effectively.

What makes someone a good communicator? There's no mystery here, since Aristotle identified the three critical elements — ethos, pathos, and logos — thousands of years ago. At the end of the day, pathos has the greatest influence on followers' perception of their leader's effectiveness as a communicator.

- Ethos is essentially your credibility — that is, the reason people should believe what you're saying.
- Pathos is making an emotional connection — essentially, the reason people believe that what you're saying will matter to them.

- Logos is your mode for appealing to others' sense of reason, ergo the term *logic*.

Ten Successful Characteristics of Leaders

1. **Accept and Give Constructive Criticism** – Sometimes leaders have to tell the truth and give the correct direction to followers---even if the followers do not want to hear it. Taking criticism will tell you a great deal about a person---let them express themselves and listen carefully.
2. **Failure is an Option** – Unfortunately, some leaders will fail. If you do, get right back up and try again. Rewards for trying and innovating and creating are sometimes intrinsic.
3. **Delegate** – We look at our role and know that it is to serve others, especially our followers, and do it with the whole person in mind.
4. **Decision-making is Key** – Make quick and effective decisions and stand behind them---whether they are right or wrong.
5. **Emphasize Diversity as Positive Interactions for Everyone** – People have so much to give from their culture and upbringing; let them offer all of what they know to help you lead while helping them succeed.
6. **Praise in Public Reprimand in Private** – Remember the stage in which you lead because you are always on stage.
7. **Manage Crisis by being Proactive** – Practice crisis management by preparing in advance and setting up

appropriate contingency plans for any and all types of crises.
8. **Take Initiative, Create, and Innovate** – Develop your skills set and continuously improve and spread it like wildfire---with no negative contention that wildfire brings.
9. **Develop the Highest Integrity** – Always remember that everything you do matters---both on and off the job.
10. **Always Teach and Learn** – Every opportunity with a follower is a teaching opportunity and every opportunity with a follower is a learning opportunity for a leader.

Send a note to the author and let him know how you enjoyed reading this book. Hope to hear from you soon.

***

ABOUT THE AUTHOR

Dr. Michael J. Provitera, Doctor of Business Administration, is an Associate Professor of Organizational Behavior in the D. Inez Andreas School of Business and Public Administration at Barry University, Miami, Florida USA. Michael published over 100 articles on a variety of topics in the management and leadership field and has conducted research and executive training sessions on many management issues, including executive leadership, emotional intelligence, motivation, leading change, strategic management, and management education.

www.ingramcontent.com/pod-product-compliance
Lightning Source LLC
Chambersburg PA
CBHW020643220526
45464CB00001B/280